An Seann Taigh

An Seann Taigh

A History of the Old Glebe House at Pipers Cove

Photographed by
ROCHELLE MACQUEEN

Written by
M. G. MADER

First published February 2024 by

DOWNINGFIELD PRESS PROPRIETARY LIMITED

www.downingfield.com · mail@downingfield.com

Suite 346 / 585 Little Collins Street 330 Avenue Avro
Melbourne Victoria 3000 Pointe-Claire Québec H9R 5W5
Australia Canada

All photographs copyright © ROCHELLE MACQUEEN 2021, 2024, unless otherwise specified. All other photographs copyright © the listed photographer unless listed as being in the public domain. All text copyright © M. G. MADER 2024. Typesetting and book design copyright © Downingfield Press Proprietary Limited 2024. All Rights Reserved.

The moral rights of the author and photographer have been asserted.

Without limiting the rights under copyright reserved above, in accordance with the Copyright Act 1968 (Commonwealth of Australia) no part of this publication may be reproduced, stored in or introduced into a retrieval system, or transmitted, in any form or by any means (electronic, mechanical, xerographic, recording, or otherwise), without the prior written permission of the copyright owner and the publisher of this book, except for brief quotes or passages used in reviews of the work.

Although the publisher and the author have made every effort to ensure that the information in this book was correct at press time and while this publication is designed to provide accurate information in regard to the subject matter covered, the publisher and the author assume no responsibility for errors, inaccuracies, omissions, or any other inconsistencies herein and hereby disclaim any liability to any party for any loss, damage, or disruption caused by errors or omissions, whether such errors or omissions result from negligence, accident, or any other cause.

Downingfield Press undertakes its work on the unceded lands of the Wurundjeri people of the Kulin Nation and pays respect to Elders past, present, and emerging.

ISBN 978-0-9959217-4-0 (HARDBACK)
ISBN 978-1-7782878-0-0 (PAPERBACK – COLOUR)
ISBN 978-1-7782878-1-7 (PAPERBACK – BLACK AND WHITE)

Cover and book design by M. G. MADER. Cover photograph copyright © M. G. MADER 2021, 2024. Half-title image by A. F. CHURCH *Map of Cape Breton County* in public domain.

A joint Australian-Canadian publication.

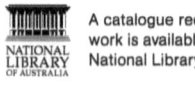 A catalogue record for this work is available from the National Library of Australia

for Jennifer

About the Contributors

ALSO BY M. G. MADER

THE END OF AN ERA
A Portrait of the Former Nova Scotian Town of Canso

THE LOCAL ELECTRIC LIGHT UTILITY
A Survey of Collectively-owned Local Electric Utilities in America and Opportunities for Australia

POWER TO THE PEOPLE
A New Model for Collective Ownership to Increase the Democratic and Sustainable Nature of Electrical Utilities

ROCHELLE MACQUEEN
Photographer

M. G. MADER
Author

ROCHELLE MACQUEEN is a Canadian photographer. She uses photography as a creative outlet to appreciate beauty in all the little things. An old decoration on a wall or aged wallpaper, peeling up to reveal the previous layers underneath, can tell a story. Rochelle enjoys finding those details and capturing them in a moment in time. She believes that pictures can help us keep precious memories in our hearts when our minds may forget the details. Decorations may be replaced, wallpaper may be removed or covered up, but photographs help us to remember the beauty of what once was long after it is gone.

M. G. MADER is a Canadian-Australian writer and town planner. He has authored three previous books. He has a strong interest in history, local governance, and politics. He works in local government within the Victorian planning system and is also managing director of Downingfield Press. He divides his time between writing, publishing, and town planning. He studied at the Royal Melbourne Institute of Technology and Cape Breton University. He lives with his husband in Melbourne.

www.mgmader.com.au

Acknowledgements

I must first thank my partner in this project, Rochelle MacQueen, without whom this book would not have been possible.

I also wish to sincerely thank all those who assisted with my research for this project, including but not limited to (but in no particular order) Pauline MacLean, archivist at Baile nan Gàidheal (Highland Village) in Iona, Nova Scotia; Debbra Wilkinson of the Geographic Names Program, Government Services Branch, Service Nova Scotia and Internal Services within the Nova Scotian government; Basil MacLean, who provided invaluable information about his relative Donald Boniface 'Dan B.' MacNeil, including photographs of the house from the 1930s and '40s; Jeff Ramsay for his photographs of the shadow box and the background history of this object; Debbie Doyle, who helped connect me to locals with historical knowledge that was invaluable to this book; Barbara Buckle for sharing information about the history of St Barra Parish; Jeanne Mader who assisted with my many queries; Lisa Ramsay, who found the invoice for the works to the house from 1985; Tracy Lenfesty, Librarian at the Natural Sciences Library, Department of Natural Resources within the Nova Scotian government; Jane Arnold, archivist at the Beaton Institute at Cape Breton University in Sydney, Nova Scotia; the very patient librarians that I pestered for microfilm and newspaper clippings at the James McConnell Memorial Library in Sydney, Nova Scotia; my many aunts, uncles, and other relatives who regaled me with stories from the good old days during their own youthful summers at Derbywood; and last but certainly not least my husband Quincy, who persevered with me through the nearly five years[*] it took to piece this history together whilst documents and research notes slowly enveloped our shared study, and then our dining room when I ran out of room in the study.

---

[*] This project began in mid-2019 and concluded in early 2024.

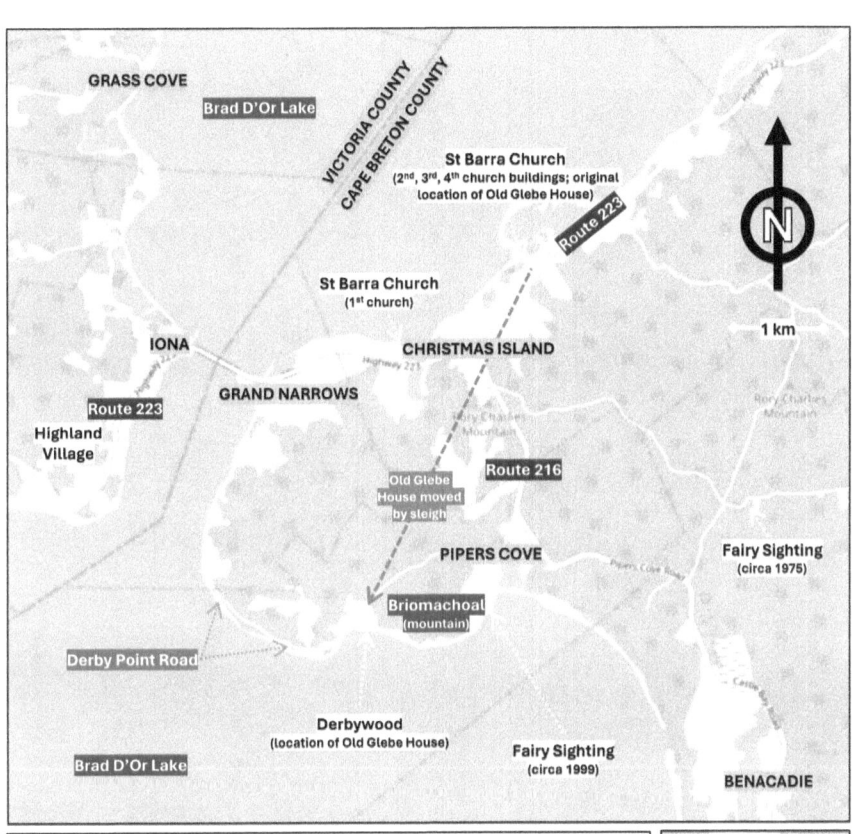

Grand Narrows and District

Introduction

There is a ritual pace to life at Derbywood; the houses are cleaned in June, the first nights spent at the weekend immediately after Grading Day, the Lobster Doo is in early July, and the Family Picnic – where all our extended kith and kin come for a day of potato sack races and tug-of-war – is the first Sunday in August. Labour Day weekend marks summer's grand finale and we close the houses for the winter, with the ritual set to be repeated come the following June.

It is a wonderful place and it has, in part, shaped me into the person I am today. I doubt I would have been as interested in history, Gaelic, or town planning if I had not been exposed to all these things, in one form or another, during my summers at Derbywood. But my family and I are simply custodians of this place. As much as we feel that we are integral to Derbywood and that Derbywood is integral to us, this place has been owned by people with whom we have no connection for most of its history. Thus, I decided to find out what stories the long history of this place holds.

This project began in 2012, when I was studying at Cape Breton University. I had taken a vernacular architecture course as an elective and I had to undertake a study of a building for my final assignment. I decided to study the house at my family's summer home, Derbywood. I spent several hours in the archives at the Beaton Institute at Cape Breton University but found very little directly relating to the house or the property. I then travelled to the archive at Highland Village – now called Baile nan Gàidheal[*] – in Iona, where I struck proverbial gold. In 1977, a postgraduate student at St Francis Xavier University had written a thesis on the history of St Barra Parish, Christmas Island and Highland Village had a copy of the paper. The paper contained information directly related to the history of the house and even mentioned that the property was now owned by a Mr Ramsay.

I wrote my paper and included some of the history, but I didn't get to explore as much of the history as I wanted. I received a good grade on the paper, and I asked if the Beaton Institute would like a copy since they had no previous records on the topic. To my delight, they warmly accepted a copy, and it remains available to researchers today. I made a mental note that I needed to return to this subject for further study in future.

Then life happened. In 2014, I was accepted at the Royal Melbourne Institute of Technology and in February 2015 I departed for Australia – permanently, as it turned out. I met my husband six months into my 'temporary' stay in Melbourne; eight years later I remain in in Melbourne and am an Australian citizen. Australia is home.

In 2019, whilst visiting Cape Breton, I was inspired[†] to continue my study of the history of Derbywood, in particular the history of the so-called 'Old House'. I then made some initial enquiries.

When I returned to Melbourne (my visit had only been a week and a half, and I hadn't had time to do research in person), I began the painstaking task of finding sources

---

[*] Literally 'village of the Gaels'.

[†] Turning my original paper into a book was originally suggested by Sara Buckle many years ago.

available on the Internet*. The pandemic struck six months later, and Melbourne had the world's longest lockdown.† I decided to make good use of my time stuck inside our home‡ by getting serious about this project. It was slow going indeed. Many archives were shut and those that were open seemed severely understaffed. I recall writing to Saint Francis Xavier University's library asking for a file that had a broken link on their website, only to be told that they knew the link was broken, they didn't have a solution, and that I should visit them in person if I wanted to see the document.§ The research took so long that the link ended up being fixed on their website about a year later and I was finally able to see the document.

I had taken a set of detailed photographs of the inside and outside of the house back in 2012. Sadly, the memory card that held these photographs died suddenly in the intervening years. The computer that they were backed up to was also lost suddenly when I returned from America in 2019 to find it had a swollen battery and had expanded to thrice its original size. Swollen batteries are highly dangerous, and I had to dispose of the computer immediately, losing all my data. The only copy of the original photographs that exists consists of rough photostats, unsuitable for publication.

I decided to enlist the help of my cousin, Rochelle MacQueen, who is an excellent photographer. Rochelle gladly agreed to provide photographs and I doubled down on the research side of things. I had hoped to finish this project in early 2021, but my partner and I bought a house

---

* It is amazing what you can find online today. I never would have guessed how much local history is online, largely due to the efforts of passionate volunteers who want to ensure local stories aren't lost.

† We were only released permanently from lockdown in October 2021!

‡ We were only allowed outside for one hour per day and couldn't travel more than five kilometres from our dwelling during Melbourne's lockdown.

§ I told them that I lived in Australia, so this was a less than helpful suggestion.

and the subsequent packing, moving, and unpacking ate up eight months of my free time. Then we got married in April 2023 and fell pregnant via surrogacy in July of the same year. Thus, we find ourselves at the beginning of 2024 and the project is only now coming to a close.

This history is neither comprehensive nor definitive, but rather a collection of various bits of history relevant to the house and the property. I wanted to write more about the history of the house, particularly its time as a Glebe House, but the Roman Catholic Diocese of Antigonish was wholly uncooperative and has locked up all the documentation relating to the history of St Barra Parish as if it were state secrets.[*] I wrote to two bishops, four priests, and one post mistress, all to no avail. I had a similar experience writing my book about Canso.

That being said, many people did reply to my enquiries, and I could not have written this book without them. I am eternally grateful to them for their assistance.

One of the most unexpected things to arise from this project was the discovery, or rather re-discovery, of the official name of a mountain. As you will read, the Nova Scotian government is now working to ascertain how the name of the mountain, on the slopes of which Derbywood sits, was lost between 1980 and 2020, when I made my initial enquiry. The process will take years, but it will hopefully result in something tangible coming out of this project. I look forward to the day when maps, and apps on our mobiles and computers, include this name again, as a direct result of this book being written.

I enjoyed researching for this project, and I am glad that Rochelle and I were able to put together a beautiful and informative record of this place that means so much to so

---

[*] I presume the secrecy around the documents relates to the ongoing dispute with the parishioners about the ownership of the property following the attempted closure of the church by the diocese and its subsequent reopening by the local parishioners.

many of us, but there is more to do. The history of our family and our time at Derbywood must be better recorded. I hope that one day there will be a revised edition, or a sequel, focussing on this more recent history. For now, I am pleased that there is at least a record, despite how incomplete it may be. Toward that end, I have organised for my personal papers relating to the research I conducted for this project to be placed in the archives of the Beaton Institute, freely available for all future researchers. I hope that any future researcher can save the five years I spent compiling this project and can use it as a head start to go deeper into the history without having to reinvent the wheel.

M. G. Mader
Melbourne, January 2024

On the slopes of
Briomachoal

The Nova Scotian community of Pipers Cove lies at the south-western most tip of Cape Breton County, which itself consists roughly of the north-eastern quarter of Cape Breton Island. Once a relatively successful rural community boasting a government wharf, post office, and school, Pipers Cove today consists of a handful of dwellings, many used as summer homes by Sydneysiders who want to escape to the countryside. The community is bounded by Christmas Island to the north, Benacadie to the east, Bras D'Or Lake[*] to the south, and Grand Narrows to the west. Two navigable public roads run through the community: Provincial Route[†] 216 and Derby Point Road. The community takes its name from Pipers Cove, a broad cove in the east of the community bounded by Briomachoal Mountain to the west and Benacadie Point to the east. This cove is known for its long, sandy beach which was once publicly accessible by a road that has long since grown over due to government indifference and abandonment. Briomachoal Mountain is located in the centre of the

---

[*] Colloquially referred to as 'the Bras d'Or Lakes'.

[†] In Nova Scotia, 'trunk' roads are often erroneously referred to as 'routes' because roads with a similar route number shield are called 'routes' in America; roads with white shields are 'trunks' and roads with brown rectangular shields are 'routes' in Nova Scotia.

community's coastline and forms a prominent point of reference along the coast.

On the western slope of Briomachoal lies Derbywood, a large estate approximately 60 acres in area, running from a rocky beach at the coast upward to the boundary of Pipers Cove with Christmas Island in the hills to the south. It is within Derbywood that we find the subject of this book: the Old Glebe House*.

An Seann Taigh is a Scottish Gaelic phrase meaning 'the old house'. Scottish Gaelic is an appropriate language to describe the house because Gaelic was the language of the house for much of its history. Pipers Cove, along with much of rural Cape Breton, was settled in the nineteenth century by Scottish Gaels escaping the Highland Clearances. As a result, it is said that 80 per cent of Cape Bretoners can trace their lineage to a Scottish Gael. Scottish Gaelic was the third most spoken language in Canada behind English and French at the turn of the twentieth century, and Gaelic remained a language spoken widely within the community up until the last quarter of that century. Discriminatory policies of assimilation developed and implemented by Celtophobic governments both in Canada and the United Kingdom led to the rapid decline of the language in the mid-twentieth century, before government-endorsed efforts at revitalisation began on both sides of the Atlantic. Today you will find bilingual English and Gaelic road signs throughout rural Cape Breton and the northern third of mainland Nova Scotia as part of this revitalisation effort.

In Pipers Cove, Gaelic was the first language of many residents until two generations ago. It is within the context of a dominant, vibrant Gaelic-speaking community that the bulk of the history of the Old Glebe House played out. Without this explanation, the casual reader may find it

---

* This dwelling is called the 'Old House' in daily parlance but is referred to as the 'Old Glebe House' in this book due to the history of the dwelling. The title of this book, An Seann Taigh, literally translates to 'the old house'.

strange that this book contains so many presumptions about the use or significance of Gaelic. These presumptions are based on the historical fact that Gaelic – not English – was the language of everyday communication for the bulk of the district's history since European settlement began.

The English language only became the dominant language spoken in the house in 1962 when W. L. Ramsay acquired the property. The mother tongue of the late Donald Boniface MacNeil (known as 'Dan B.') was Gaelic, according to the 1911 Canadian Census, and is it Gaelic that most likely would have been spoken in the house prior to 1962.

For most of the dwelling's two centuries of existence, it was Gaelic and not English that was to be heard within its walls. And one can't help but wonder what stories the walls would tell if they could talk. The have witnessed nearly the full span of European settlement and development in this part of Nova Scotia.

A New World
An Old Religion

Fifteen millennia ago North America was covered in enormous glaciers, but it was about this time that they began to retreat. So much water was held in those glaciers that the sea level was significantly lower than it is today. As a result, there was no Prince Edward Island or Cape Breton Island – they were just coastal edges of mainland North America covered in ice kilometres deep. But 15,000 years ago those mammoth glaciers began to recede across North America. As the glaciers melted, the sea levels rose, and the land literally sprang upward as it was released from the weight of the melting ice. The glaciers did not melt consistently as the ice was thicker in some places than in others. In northeastern North America, the glaciers receded towards the middle of what is now Cape Breton Island and the melting ice formed a lake that drained northward toward the then-much lower ocean. As the glaciers melted all over the world, the oceans rose and eventually the sea came flooding back inland towards the fresh water lake in the centre of Cape Breton Island, forming an unique inland sea of brackish water. This inland sea would form an important ecosystem over the next few millennia, eventually creating the Bras D'Or Lake that we know today.

Around four millennia ago, people arrived and settled along the edges of this inland sea. The Mi'kmaq people settled what is now the Maritimes region of Canada and called it *Mi'kma'ki*. They made Cape Breton, which they called *Unama'ki*, the capital of *Mi'kma'ki* – the seat of the Grand Council.* † They settled predominantly along the waters of the Bras D'Or Lake – *Pitupaq* in the Mi'kmaq language, meaning 'long salt water'. Over the next 3500 years, the Mi'kmaq developed a distinctive culture and connection to the land.

In the middle of the last millennium, Europeans made contact with the Mi'kmaq as they began to colonise North America. As early as 1650, a French trading post was established along the shores of the great inland sea and the lake was given a European name *Le Lac de Labrador* or, sometimes, *Labrador*,‡ a name of Portuguese origin meaning 'farmer' that was given to much of what would eventually become eastern Canada. In the eighteenth century, the French established a fortress at Louisbourg and by the turn of the nineteenth century, the British had successfully won all of eastern Canada from the French (bar St-Pierre and Miquelon) and Yankees (followed by Loyalists escaping the rebellion and bloodshed in the newly independent United States) had settled at and established Sydney. Now British immigrants were beginning to trickle into the new Colony of Cape Breton, mostly Scots who were being forced off their ancestral land by the powerful landowners who were replacing tenant farmers with more profitable sheep.

---

* 'Mi'kmaq', Intercontinental Cry, Retrieved 2 December 2016.

† In 2020, following more than a century of the Grand Council being relegated to a solely spiritual organisation, the Government of Canada recognised the Grand Council's role in Mi'kmaq society and provided authorisation for the Council to consult and advise government on behalf of the Mi'kmaq people.

‡ 'Chart of the Gulf of St Lawrence, Composed from a Great Number of Actual Surveys – David Rumsey Historical Map Collection', Sayer and Bennet, London, 1708.

Until the Highlanders' loss at Culloden in 1746, the Highlands of Scotland were governed under the ancient clan system. The victory of the English in that year had far reaching implications for the Highlander people as the imposition of English laws, culture, and traditions meant complete upheaval in the lives of the common folk.* The changes included the deprivation of power from the traditional clan chieftains; the banning of the wearing of tartan, kilts, and the playing of bagpipes. Traditional ways of life broke down. The chieftan became landlord, rather than chief – leader and protector of the clan. The chieftains moved from the Highlands to the Lowlands or London and lived in relative luxury on the profits earnt from their clansmens' work – who were their tenant farmers after 1746. The chieftains would eventually develop into the Scottish nobility. Some Highlanders, particularly those with the means of doing so, left Scotland for the New World voluntarily in the years after the loss at Culloden. Others entered into indentured service, whereby a wealthy colonial would pay for the Scot's voyage across the Atlantic in exchange for seven years free labour.†

By 1815, the price of wool rose dramatically. The chieftain landlords, who had been absent from the Highlands for half a century, were looking for ways to increase the profit of their landholdings. They did this by forcefully evicting the tenant farmers – their clansmen – from their tenant farms and replacing them with sheep. The Highlanders were mostly forced to leave the British Isles due to poor economic conditions and lack of opportunity; the Scottish Clearances had begun in earnest. The large Scottish diaspora in the former British Empire – Australia, Canada, New Zealand, South Africa – as well as the United States is due in great part to the forced evictions of the Highlanders at this time.

---

* Interestingly, it was the already much-Anglicised Lowland Scots who were responsible for implementing much of the cultural destruction as they acted on behalf of the English.

† The song Amazing Grace is about an indentured servant.

Although Scottish culture and Nova Scotia (Cape Breton in particular) are inseparable today, this was not always the case. The first Scottish immigrants to Cape Breton directly from Scotland did not arrive until 1802, two centuries after the beginning of the colonisation of the island. These first immigrants were Gaelic speaking Highlanders and consisted of both Roman Catholics and Presbyterians. There was already a growing concentration of Catholic Gaels in northern mainland Nova Scotia centred on Antigonish, whilst immigrants arriving at Pictou were predominantly Presbyterian. The situation in Cape Breton was mixed and would remain so, although Gaels tended to settle areas along sectarian lines.* Catholic Gaels who arrived at Pictou were often persuaded to permanently settle elsewhere in the province in areas with larger Catholic Gael populations.

It was in 1802 that 370 Highlander Gaels arrived at Pictou from the Isle of Barra in the Outer Hebrides of Scotland. Being islanders, they were settled on Pictou Island at the direction of Governor Wentworth.† Later in the year, the a group of Barramen – all Catholics – sailed to Cape Breton and up into the Bras D'Or to the Grand Narrows‡ where they cleared the land and planted crops during the summer. After the harvest, they returned to winter in Pictou. The same men returned to the district for the summer again in 1803, before returning to settle permanently in 1804.§ About twenty Barra families settled in the Grand Narrows district.¶

---

* The Gaelic language survived longer amongst Roman Catholic Gaels than Presbyterian Gaels, especially in more remote settlements.

† Wentworth was the governor of mainland Nova Scotia – the Colony of Nova Scotia – as Cape Breton was a separate British colony from the 1780s through 1820. The independent Colony of Cape Breton was abolished at the urging of Halifax interests who wanted to take advantage of the island's large coal reserves.

‡ Later to be called Barra Strait after these first settlers.

§ One man died between 1803 and 1804.

¶ Grand Narrows referred in the first years of settlement to both the Cape Breton County and Victoria County side of the strait; the name

These were the first Europeans to settle in central Cape Breton, along the shores of that great inland sea: the Bras D'Or Lake.*

The Roman Catholics who settled the Grand Narrows district were from Barra in the Outer Hebrides in Scotland; a remote area so far removed from civilisation and so infrequently visited that it is described as 'the island that the Reformation did not reach'.† Its people, the Barramen, continued on the last remnants of the pre-Reformation Scottish Catholicism tradition. Most Scots are Presbyterian; the Barramen, alongside the people of neighbouring South Uist, are predominantly Roman Catholic and all of the Barramen that settled in the Grand Narrows district were Roman Catholic.‡ As late as 2011, South Uist was still 90 per cent Catholic and Barra was still 81.5 per cent Catholic.§ Prior to the arrival of Christianity, the Outer Hebrides were host to some of Great Britain's most sacred religious sites, some dating as far back as five millennia. In the late sixth century, St Barra¶ visited the Isle of Barra and gave the island its name. St Barra was the Bishop of Cork in Ireland, where Christianity had established itself around 400 AD. St Columba established a monastery on the Isle of Iona in 563 AD and a small Catholic chapel was then planted in Barra in the eighth century as a branch of the

---

Iona was not adopted until later in the nineteenth century.

* The official name is Bras D'Or Lake, but most Cape Bretoners call it the Bras D'Or Lakes and, indeed, the lake is officially broken down into sections such as Great Bras D'Or Channel, East Bay, St Patrick's Channel, West Bay, Whycogomagh Bay, Nyanza Bay, and St Andrew's Channel.

† Sheilds, Tom, 'Island the Reformation did not reach', Glasgow Herald, 10 March 1982.

‡ Indeed there are no Protestant churches in the Grand Narrows district whatsoever, nor have any ever existed, but you will find three Roman Catholic churches within a 30 minute drive.

§ National Records of Scotland, 2011 Census, Table Number KS209SCb.

¶ Also known as St Barr or St Finbarr.

Iona monastery. The people of Barra would remember and revere both St Barra and St Columba for more than a millennium before bringing their names with them to the New World. The first parish established in the Grand Narrows district by the newly arrived Barramen was called St Barra Church; three-quarters of a century later, when a new church was established on the Victoria County side of the Barra Strait, the parish was named St Columba Church.

The first decade that the Barramen spent in the Grand Narrows district was primitive; nothing but thick forest existed when they arrived and survival against the elements dominated the first few years of European settlement. The first priority for new settlers was to clear enough land to grow a small crop in order to feed themselves and their families for that first winter. Rudimentary single room log cabins were hastily constructed out of the lumber from the cleared trees and hearty vegetables such as potatoes were planted amongst the still-present tree stumps. It would be a year or two of hard toil before the stumps could be cleared, and it had to be done by hand with the help of horses. No community facilities existed. There were no schools or churches or civic institutions in this new community. Even in Sydney, the capital of the small Colony of Cape Breton, only basic civic institutions existed: a barracks, a small government house, a cluster of houses, and a shop or two.

An excerpt from *A Brief History of Christmas Island Parish 1814-1996* provides insight into the enormity of the task that faced the settlers when they arrived in the district:

About twenty families arrived and ten settled on each side of the Narrows. When the pioneers came here, it was all forest to the edge of the water. There was a great task before them to clear the forest, till the soil and build themselves homes. As the population increased and being of strong Catholic faith, they decided to build a log cabin church and house in case a priest should come at any time to visit them.

The first Barramen arrived at Grand Narrows in 1802 and settled permanently there in 1804; it was not until 1814-15 that the settlers had established themselves enough to turn their mind to community institutions. When they did this, the first institution was a place of worship. The first church – called St Barra – was a small, primitive log cabin, without windows, constructed near Coopers Pond where the Intercolonial Railway would later be built.[*] It was said that debris from the first church could be seen sticking out of the back fill used to build the embankment for the line.[†] A smaller log cabin was erected alongside the church as a glebe house[‡] for a priest, although it would be five years before a priest would take up residence in the district. St Barra was the first Catholic church built along the shores of the Bras D'Or. The railway was built 75 years after the original first church, so it is unlikely that the primitive and rudimentary buildings built in 1814-15 were still standing at that time, but the ruins would have likely been strewn about the site where they had once stood.

The first log church was built on the shore a mile below the strait, just below the present cemetery. Its size was 35' by 20'. It was so close to the beach that at high tide the water would rise under it, but without doing any harm to the flooring, for the chapel was built on bricks. When completed this chapel was to have two windows, but no place was cut out for them as yet. The only light for inside came through the open door and through the open spaces between the logs. These spaces were caulked with moss, but some of it had fallen out.[§]

---

[*] Eventually absorbed into the Canadian National Railways (CN) and then privatised and sold off in the 1990s as the Cape Breton and Central Nova Scotia Railway.

[†] For the Love of St Barra, Pedalling Prince Productions, 2016.

[‡] Glebe house is a term used to denote the house provided by the church for a Roman Catholic parish priest; it is the same as a manse in the Presbyterian tradition and a vicarage in the Anglican tradition.

[§] Clan MacNeil and Christmas Island Historical Society, A Brief History of Christmas Island Parish 1814-1996, 1996.

This passage illuminates the extremely primitive nature of the first church and underlines why a replacement was required after only a decade of service. It also lends support for the theory that the second glebe house being constructed around the time of the second church; if the log church was worn out, it stands to reason that the primitive log glebe house was also worn out.

A legacy of the first church being located at Coopers Pond, not at Christmas Island like later churches, is the St Barra parish cemetery being located just up the hill from the original church site in what is now MacNeils Road, Christmas Island. A memorial at the site of the first church reads:

At this site stood the Highland Settlers' first Catholic church on the Bras D'Or Lakes 1824 CR. The Reverend Willliam Dollard was the first resident priest, 1820, from this mission spread the beginning of higher learning in the Diocese of Antigonish, 1824. Erected by Clan MacNeil, 1996, Atlantic Provinces Branch.

The first church was occasionally visited by passing priests in the years between its construction and the arrival of the first resident priest. But for the most part the people of the district were unable to take the sacraments central to their faith.

In June of 1815, the Bishop – all the way from Quebec – visited the rudimentary chapel. The visit from Wednesday, 28 June through Friday, 30 June did not go smoothly as the Bishop spoke only French and the parishioners of the district spoke only Gaelic. The Bishop and his accompanying party were warmly welcomed, but he could not administer the sacraments in a language that could be understood by his flock and thus the flock were unable to partake in the rituals. Upon returning from his visit, the Bishop understood with new vigour the importance of finding a parish priest for these devout Catholics and set about trying to find one that could speak Gaelic.

As the chapel was recently constructed, there was nothing in it for the celebration of mass. They had to bring everything with them.

[The Bishop] wanted to say an edifying word to [the parishioners] in English, but not one of his assistants could translate it into Gaelic, so he had to be silent.

The rosary and vespers were recited aloud in the presence of some twenty Highlanders who understood nothing of either. This was followed by spiritual reading in French, of which they understood less, and during it [the parishioners] left, one after another.

The failure of the Bishop and his priests to administer the sacraments to any of the 100 families of Highlanders settled at Christmas Island and at other places around the Bras D'Or Lake was due to the clerics' inability to speak Gaelic.

The Bishop...determined to renew his efforts to find a priest to whose care he might soon confide these unintentionally neglected members of his vast flock; but nearly three years were to go by before he succeeded.[*]

It was sixteen years after their permanent settlement in the district that the first resident priest arrived. In 1820, the Reverend William Dollard arrived in Christmas Island to serve as the parish's first resident priest, but he stayed only a short time. He fell ill and was forced to leave after only a year at Christmas Island.[†] He made a full recovery but never returned to St Barra or the Grand Narrows district.

---

[*] Clan MacNeil and Christmas Island Historical Society, A Brief History of Christmas Island Parish 1814-1996, 1996.

[†] Grand Narrows district, as used in this book, refers to the modern communities of Grand Narrows (Cape Breton County), Christmas Island, Pipers Cove, and Iona (which was known initially as Grand Narrows, Victoria County before acquiring its own identity). St Barra Church is located in Christmas Island, which is only a few kilometres from the modern-day community of Grand Narrows.

William Dollard was the first of three Williams who would be parish priest at St Barra Church. The Reverend William Fraser arrived to take up the post in 1822, but stayed in Christmas Island only nine months before departing to another posting. He would later be ordained Bishop of Antigonish in 1827.

Eighteen months after the departure of William Fraser, the third William – Reverend William MacLeod – arrived as joint parish priest for both St Barra Church and the Catholic church at East Bay. He divided his time equally between the two communities, and it was under his tenure that the church stabilised and began to build a legacy in the local community.* † In 1823, William Fraser had organised the commencement of the construction of a new frame church at Christmas Island to replace the rapidly ageing, temporary log structure. William MacLeod oversaw the completion of this new church. The new frame church was completed in 1824. Unlike its predecessor, the new frame church was built a kilometre to the north near Christmas Island, just north and towards the shore of where the present church stands.‡

William MacLeod also organised the first training programme for future priests in what would eventually become the Diocese of Antigonish, when he gathered nine young men and began educating them in the art and science of the priesthood. His training programme eventually garnered the name of 'The College' and became a minor seminary.

The new school was known locally as 'The College' and its importance lies in the fact that it was a minor seminary and the first institution in the present Diocese of Antigonish in

---

* 'Our Bishop, List of Bishops', Diocese of Antigonish, accessed 21 August 2022.

† A. K. MacKenzie, History of Christmas Island Parish, 1926, pp. 5-6.

‡ The present church is the fourth church, constructed after the third church burnt down in 1972.

which young men were given their preliminary training for ecclesiastical state.

Five of these students became priests, and one of them, MacKinnon, became the second bishop of the diocese. Father MacLeod's educational plan was continued and expanded by MacKinnon, who established the St Andrew's Grammar School and later the Diocesan College which is now St Francis Xavier University. [*]

The training programme set up by William MacLeod, parish priest at St Barra Church in Christmas Island, was run in the church building and, very likely, in his personal residence, the glebe house. Eventually a school was constructed at East Bay[†], but it began with Father MacLeod, who was shuttling back and forth between East Bay and Christmas Island. The history of the construction of the second church supports the theory that the second glebe house was in existence at the time that William MacLeod was priest at Christmas Island. Therefore, it is very likely that the earliest educational institution in the Diocese of Antigonish was established and undertaken in the second glebe house at Christmas Island. That is to say, the institution that would eventually develop into the Diocesan College and then into St Francis Xavier University began at Christmas Island in the second glebe house – the Old Glebe House, which is the subject of this book.

It is very likely that a new frame glebe house was also constructed at the same time or very soon after the construction of a frame church; if the log church needed replacement, it stands to reason that the log glebe house – only ever intended to be temporary – also needed replacement, as both buildings were nearing the ten year

---

[*] Clan MacNeil and Christmas Island Historical Society, A Brief History of Christmas Island Parish 1814-1996, 1996.

[†] St Barra Church in Christmas Island and the Catholic church at East Bay shared a parish priest during the early years of European settlement.

mark. We also know that the second church was built some distance from the original log church, and in the days before the automobile it is very unlikely that the priest would have continued to dwell at Coopers Pond, in what was by all accounts an extremely primitive structure located far away from his new church and so close to the water's edge that the high tide swelled up under the building, nearly touching the floorboards. No written records say whether a new glebe house was indeed constructed at this time, but based on the architectural style of the building (which still stands today), as well as the range of dates in the records for the construction of the first and third glebe houses, the theory that a second glebe house was constructed at the same time or very soon after the construction of the second church is very likely. An 1877 map of Cape Breton County showing the names of all of the residents beside each and every dwelling in the county includes a notation showing a glebe house next to the location of the second church in Christmas Island.[*] Thus, we know that a glebe house was built sometime in the nineteenth century to replace the original log glebe house at Coopers Pond. The third glebe house was built in 1896[†], so it stands to reason that the second glebe house was likely built at the same time or very soon after the second church, otherwise it would not have been old enough to warrant replacement in the 1890s.

The location of the second church was closer to the water than the current church and slightly to the north, in an area lightly wooded in present day. A depression in the ground can still be found at the site of the second church.[‡] Originally the road through Christmas Island ran much closer to the shoreline, and traces of its route can still be seen in aerial imagery. The 1877 map shows that the second

---

[*] A. F. Church, Map of Cape Breton County, 1877 (obtained from the Nova Scotian Department of Natural Resources Library in Halifax by post in 2019).

[†] It burnt in 1926 and was replaced by the current glebe house in 1927.

[‡] For the Love of St Barra, Pedalling Prince Productions, 2016.

church was on a small lane off the old road and thus much closer to the shoreline than the third and fourth churches and glebe houses. There was at one time a steam boat landing in Christmas Island and this is also shown on the 1877 map; the second church is shown just inland, on the same small lane as the steam boat landing, and the glebe house appears to be inland from this adjacent to the main road.

Three images – one from the very early twentieth century and another likely from the 1920s – shows a panoramic view of Christmas Island. One photo is black and white and appears to be considerably older than the other two. It is possible to date the photos because the 1896 glebe house, a very distinctive building, is shown prominently in all three. In two of these photos, a house can be seen near the marshland and creek that separate the churchyard from the rest of the community. This house has a distinctive fenestration* that matches that of the second glebe house. The shape of the building is also distinctive and aligns with that of the second glebe house. Multiple sources have confirmed that the second glebe house was acquired by Donald Boniface "Dan B." MacNeil in the early twentieth century, who bought the building but not the land and moved the house to his ancestral property at Pipers Cove. We thus know what the second glebe house looks like, but all the records focus on the church buildings and the original location of the second glebe house and the year it was acquired by Dan B. MacNeil are unknown. The dwelling that appears in these three photos matches the appearance of the second glebe house and it has the distinctive off-centre fenestration of windows that is a key feature of the second glebe house (the house that is the focus of this book). Moreover, the location of the dwelling – which does not match the appearance of any other dwellings known to have existed in that area – aligns with the location of the glebe house on the 1877 map of Cape Breton County discussed above. It is possible that the

---

* The arrangement of windows in a building facade.

Two early twentieth century photographs showing St Barra Church, the 1896 glebe house, and – in the foreground – a small house with similiar characteristics to the Old Glebe House at Derbywood.
PHOTOGRAPHS IN PUBLC DOMAIN

dwelling shown in these photos may be the second glebe house* and that these photos were taken before Dan B. MacNeil acquired the house and relocated it to its present location in Pipers Cove.

Administratively, Cape Breton – which was joined with the Colony of Nova Scotia after losing its independence as a British Colony in 1820 – was separated from the Diocese of Quebec and joined with the Catholic administrative organisation in Nova Scotia in 1829. Nine years later in 1838, at a local level, East Bay and Christmas Island parishes were separated into parishes in their own right. In 1837, the school established some years earlier by Rev. MacLeod at Christmas Island and East Bay began to produce results, as one of the students was ordained into the priesthood and appointed to serve as parish priest at St Barra Church. He was appointed to Christmas Island specifically because he spoke Gaelic. Finally, a supply of

---

* A Christmas Island local contacted me to say she thought the house belonged to someone else, but these photos were taken well before this person's mother was born, meaning the photos are two generations older than this person and this person is therefore not a firsthand, or even secondhand, witness. Moreover, the oldest of the photos appears to show the house sitting near the church before many of the houses in Christmas Island were built. I believe this oldest photo was taken only a few years after the construction of the 1896 third glebe house and that the photos show the second glebe house, which was moved to Pipers Cove by Dan B. MacNeil shortly after the photos were taken. I further believe that the house the person thought was shown in the photograph was constructed at a later date near the same location. I make this educated guess on the basis that: several independent sources say the house at Pipers Cove was moved from Christmas Island and was originally the glebe house of St Barra Church; the fenestration and shape of the house shown is remarkably close to that of the house at Pipers Cove, especially if one considers that the porch would have been added after the house was moved to Pipers Cove; and finally, the 1877 map shows the location of the third glebe house being located in the same location that the photograph shows the house in question, therefore it is a very logical leap to presume that the house in the photograph is the same house as that in Pipers Cove.

Gaelic speaking priests was coming on the line to serve the Catholic Gaels of Cape Breton and Nova Scotia.[*]

[The] successor at Grand Narrows was Father John Grant, one of the charter students of the 'East Bay College'. He was ordained in 1837, and was well suited to the Grand Narrows Parish, especially because of the 'powerful Gaelic sermons' which he preached.[†]

John Grant established a small log church in Boisdale in 1840, near the site of the magnificent present-day stone church. A small glebe was also built at the time. Mirroring the experience of the mother church at Christmas Island, it was years before a permanent parish priest was available and appointed to serve only at Boisdale.[‡]

The parishioners of St Barra Church were treated to the rare event of having the Bishop of Antigonish serve as interim parish priest for a few weeks after Easter in 1854, following the departure of a number of parish priest appointees in short succession for a number of reasons, including one who fell ill with tuberculosis.[§]

Originally known as the 'Grand Narrows Church' or 'Grand Narrows Parish', the first record of the name St Barra Church did not occur until 1853. The name 'St Barra' is a Nova Scotian invention, the Scottish know this saint as St Barr or St Finbarr.

---

[*] Clan MacNeil and Christmas Island Historical Society, A Brief History of Christmas Island Parish 1814-1996, 1996.

[†] Clan MacNeil and Christmas Island Historical Society, A Brief History of Christmas Island Parish 1814-1996, 1996.

[‡] Clan MacNeil and Christmas Island Historical Society, A Brief History of Christmas Island Parish 1814-1996, 1996.

[§] Clan MacNeil and Christmas Island Historical Society, A Brief History of Christmas Island Parish 1814-1996, 1996.

*...St Barra, evidently a Nova Scotia variant of St Barr or Finbar [sic], and this form of name has remained.**

St Barra Church was also the mother church of Catholics in Baddeck until they completed their church in 1858.† As the population in Cape Breton began to grow rapidly, now six decades since the arrival of the first Scots in Cape Breton, new parishes in their own right were required in the many growing communities throughout Cape Breton. The frontier was settled and pioneers had established communities, which now required community institutions.

The people on both sides of the Barra Strait worshipped at St Barra in Christmas Island during the first decades of European settlement. It was not until 1859‡ that a church was built at Sundrie (now called Iona)§ on the west side of the strait. When both communities worshipped at St Barra Church, it was not uncommon to see twenty or thirty rowboats beached below the church; this was the mode of transport for those who travelled across the strait for Sunday mass. In 1873, Iona was separated from Christmas Island into a parish of its own, with Baddeck falling under the new Iona parish. Christmas Island remained its own parish with only the one church, allowing the parish priest to focus on tending to his own local flock.

And tend to their flock they did; in 1909 Reverend Angus R. MacDonald was appointed to serve as parish priest at

---

* Clan MacNeil and Christmas Island Historical Society, A Brief History of Christmas Island Parish 1814-1966, 1996.

† Construction began in 1851 and took until 1858 to be completed.

‡ Construction began in 1857.

§ Originally named Grand Narrows, Victoria County, the twin to Grand Narrows, Cape Breton County, the community was later renamed Sundrie and then renamed again to its current name, Iona. The Gaelic name for the community is Sanndraigh; it was not changed when Sundrie became Iona in English.

Christmas Island. He remained there for 43 years and was to start a tradition of long-serving parish priests that would last much of the twentieth century. In 1913, he led the establishment of the Christmas Island Co-Op Association. He also spearheaded the replacement of the glebe house in 1926, when the 1896 glebe burnt down.* Angus MacDonald was buried at Christmas Island when he died in 1953. He was followed by Reverend Alexander A. Ross, who served for many decades as parish priest at Christmas Island.†

The Christmas Island Co-Op Association was likely the first cooperative in Cape Breton, well ahead of the Antigonish Movement that would follow in later decades. It was originally called 'The Farmer's Association' but the name was changed in 1916. The impetus for the formation of the cooperative was greedy profiteering by some merchants upon the outbreak of the First World War.‡

The large wholesale merchants seized upon [the war] as an opportunity to make a 'fast buck'. They inflated prices on their inventory as much as 50 to 100% on some items. The small stores around the country were at their mercy. Consequently, everyone felt the pinch.§

This became a common topic of conversation locally and it was brought up at a St Barra Parish League of the Cross meeting, which was a very active community organisation at the time. The people of the parish took upon themselves the task of issuing a 'declaration of war on profiteering'. A committee was established to look into the issue and seek

---

* Clan MacNeil and Christmas Island Historical Society, A Brief History of Christmas Island 1814-1996, 1996.

† Clan MacNeil and Christmas Island Historical Society, A Brief History of Christmas Island 1814-1996, 1996.

‡ Archibald MacKenzie, The MacKenzies' History of Christmas Island Parsh, 1983, pp.246.

§ Archibald MacKenzie, The MacKenzies' History of Christmas Island Parsh, 1983, pp.246.

solutions to help protect the local shops and their customers from price gouging.*

The executive were given a mandate to study the problem and come up with an idea that might help to alleviate the hardship the people were forced to endure. They held a meeting in our kitchen...I was only 7 years of age, I remember the discussion quite vividly. It was practically all in Gaelic, which gave me an advantage as my knowledge of the English language was limited at that time. The one who impressed me the most was Rory MacKinnon from Castle Bay...he rose waving his fist and spoke as eloquently as some of the great promoters of the Co-op movement, who came along many years later.†

The committee reported their discussions and ideas to the parish priest, Angus MacDonald, who took on the role of organising the movement. A meeting was held and the community formed the cooperative for the mutual benefit of all community members.

The third church was built in 1883 almost exactly at the location of the present day (fourth) church. The exterior was constructed by a contracted builder, but the interior was finished by local parishioners. The third church was destroyed by fire on 2 December 1972, 89 years after its construction. The *Cape Breton Post* from Monday, 4 December 1972 reads:

Fire Saturday destroyed St Barra's Roman Catholic Church at Christmas Island. The Church, which dates back to 1883, replaced an older church at Christmas Island. Prior to the construction of the original church on the island, parishioners were served by a small church at Coopers

---

* Archibald MacKenzie, The MacKenzies' History of Christmas Island Parsh, 1983, pp.247.

† Archibald MacKenzie, The MacKenzies' History of Christmas Island Parsh, 1983, pp.247.

Island [sic].* Saturday's fire is believed to have originated in the vicinity of the furnace. Fanned by high winds, flames spread quickly in the wooden structure. Through valiant efforts, men of the parish managed to save the Holy Eucharist, vestments, linens, and sanctuary furnishings. Iona Fire Department was first on the scene but the fire was already too advanced to be brought under control.† Sydney River, Coxheath, and Mira Road answered the call but by the time they arrived the most they could do was to water the smouldering ruins.‡ ... Rev. A. A. Ross, pastor of St Barra said there was considerable insurance on the structure, which he valued at well over $100,000.§ ¶

The Reverend A. A. Ross mentioned in the article was Father Alexander A. Ross, who came to St Barra on 9 September 1952 and would eventually be fairly well known to W. L. Ramsay and his children. After the fire, mass was held in the parish hall until the new church was completed in 1975.# The fourth church was completed and dedicated on 17 August 1975 by Msgr W. J. Gallivan, Vicar General.** Alexander Ross was still serving as the parish priest at St Barra in 1996, when *A Brief History of Christmas Island*

---

* This should read Coopers Pond, not Coopers Island.

† Iona Fire Department would have had to call, wait for, and then travel on the Barra Strait Ferry as there was no road bridge at this time.

‡ It is understood that the Christmas Island Fire Department had not yet been established; the volunteer fire brigades now common throughout Nova Scotia were only beginning to be established in the 1970s.

§ A not inconsiderable sum in 1972.

¶ 'St Barra's Church Destroyed by Fire', Cape Breton Post, 4 December 1972.

Clan MacNeil and Christmas Island Historical Society, A Brief History of Chrismtas Island Parish 1814-1996, 1996 (available at James McConnell Memorial Library, Sydney, Nova Scotia, Canada; call number 282.7169 Bri N.S.C.)

** A Brief History of Christmas Island Parish 1814-1996 contains a succinct timeline at the end of the booklet outlining the history of the parish and its church buildings: Log Cabin: 1814-1824; Second Church: 1824-1883; Third Church: 1883-1972; Present (fourth) Church: 1975-present.

Parish 1814-1996 was published. He retried from St Barra Church in 1998; the church has the distinction of having had only two parish priests from 1909 through 1998, a remarkable feat considering how frequently priests came and went in the first century of the parish's history.*

St Barra's time as a parish in its own right – under the Roman Catholic Church, anyway – came to an end in 2013, when the Diocese of Antigonish announced it was amalgamating St Barra Parish at Christmas Island with St Columba Parish at Iona, 140 years after the two parishes had been separated into individual parishes.† The announcement was made in January 2013 following the release of a pastoral plan as part of a wider plan to rationalise the number of Catholic parishes throughout the Diocese. The church properties being closed were being sold off to raise funds. The funds were required to pay a $15 million compensation bill following the diocese reaching a settlement with victims of abuse by priests. The diocese also liquidated the bank accounts of many parishes throughout the diocese and borrowed $6.5 million.‡

The parishioners at Christmas Island, protested against the plan and the diocesan authorities granted a temporary reprieve in the closure plans, allowing the church to remain consecrated until after its 200th anniversary in 2015.

[The parishioners] were hoping that the church would open for [the 200th anniversary] and the bishop agreed with them that it is an important anniversary, not only to them, but to the diocese.§

---

* 'Man's final wish was to reopen church', Cape Breton Post, 3 March 2016.

† 'St Barra's will be open for 200th anniversary', Cape Breton Post, 27 February 2013.

‡ 'Diocese of Antigonish starts church review', The Chronicle Herald, 14 April 2014.

§ 'St Barra's will be open for 200th anniversary', Cape Breton Post, 27 February 2013.

The parishioners of Christmas Island were not satisfied, however. They noted that it was the community, not the diocese – which did not even exist at the time – that built the original church and established the parish. They also contested the diocese's ownership of the church property, noting the deed to the land was never transferred to the diocese.

The ownership of the church and the property is legally in question because we have a deed that predates the formation of the Diocese of Arichat* which predates the formation of the Diocese of Antigonish.†

In 2016, the parishioners held a meeting and decided to form a society to take control of the property and continue managing the church; in essence, they became modern day protestants as they defied the power of the local bishop and Rome – although they still see themselves as Catholic. They formed the Wardens of the Church of St Barra Preservation and Development Society and continue to operate the church, with lay preachers leading worship each Sunday. Recognised Catholic services continue across the Barra Strait at St Columba Church in Iona led by an ordained Catholic priest. The formation of the society followed an unsuccessful appeal to the Bishop of Antigonish – and ultimately to Rome – seeking to overturn to the decision to close and secularise St Barra Church.‡

It is poetic that St Barra church began as a community led church, built in hopes that a priest might come by and hold a service for the people, and has now returned to being a community led church that carries on its 210 year tradition in defiance of the powers in Antigonish and Rome who

---

* The Diocese of Arichat later became the Diocese of Antigonish when the seat of the bishop moved to Antigonish.

† 'Man's final wish was to reopen church', Cape Breton Post, 3 March 2016.

‡ 'Man's final wish was to reopen church', Cape Breton Post, 3 March 2016.

wish to see this 200 year old community closed and broken up. It's not surprising that the parishioners of St Barra took matters into their own hands when the bishop decided to close their church. They took matters into their own hands in 1814 when they built the first church, they took matters into their own hands when they formed the cooperative a century ago, and they have now taken matters into their own hands again in order to preserve their community, their tradition, and their spiritual way of life.

Dan B. (centre), Mary Ann (right), and an unidentified person. The barn located just north of the house's location as well as another barn on the northern side of Derby Point Road are visible in the background. Both barns survived until the Ramsay acquisition of the property but have since been demolished.
PHOTOGRAPH COURTESY BASIL MACLEAN

LEFT Photograph of Veronica MacLean hunting, with Derbywood beach and Briomachoal in background, circa 1947.

ABOVE *Pipers Cove in the Pasture*, 16 August 1938. Mary Ann MacNeil with 'Vonnie and Princie' with the eastern facade of the house visible in the background, including original windows and the chimney. PHOTOGRAPHS COURTESY BASIL MACLEAN

'Potbelly' style wood stove from the house at it appeared in 2012, shortly after being relocated to the out of doors and prior to its deterioration and loss. The original colour photograph was lost.
PHOTOGRAPH BY M. G. MADER

Moss-covered stones piled in the woods after being removed from a ruined foundation during the construction of the 'New House' in the 1980s. PHOTOGRAPH BY M. G. MADER

Winter view of Briomachoal (mountain), the beach at Derbywood, and the cliffs of Benacadie far off in the distance, circa 2021.
PHOTOGRAPH BY M. G. MADER

Mary Ann MacNeil with southern facade of the house visible, circa 1930s. PHOTOGRAPH COURTESY BASIL MACLEAN

Colourised photograph of George MacLean hunting on the Quinn's property with Derbywood in background, circa 1947.
PHOTOGRAPH COURTESY BASIL MACLEAN

Donald Boniface 'Dan B.' MacNeil and his wife Mary Ann MacNeil in the kitchen of the house circa 1940s or 1950s. The cupboard partially visible in the rear left remains intact within the house. The interior of the porch (demolished in 1985) is visible at the rear right.
PHOTOGRAPH COURTESY BASIL MACLEAN

Barra Strait Ferry docked at Grand Narrows circa 1902.
PUBLIC DOMAIN PHOTOGRAPH

Barra Strait railway bridge (pre-1914 span replacement) at the turn of the twentieth century. Note St Columba church in the background. PUBLIC DOMAIN PHOTOGRAPH

Views of Grand Narrows and district at the turn of the twentieth century.
PUBLIC DOMAIN PHOTOGRAPH

An Ancient People in a New Land

The area now known as Pipers Cove is known to the indigenous Mi'kmaq people as *Jakejuikuomk*, which refers not to the namesake cove but rather Derby Point, a promontory near the boundary of the modern-day communities of Pipers Cove and Grand Narrows. This name is roughly translated as 'at the lobster shack[*]'. The modern English name for the community is derived from the Gaelic name: *Cobn nam Piobairean*, literally 'cove of the pipers'. The English spelling has varied widely, occasionally being spelt differently between the three place name signs posted at the boundary of the community. When I last visited Pipers Cove, both signs on route 216 used the English spelling 'Piper's Cove' whilst the sign in Derby Point Road spelt the name 'Pipers Cove', which appears to show a discrepancy even amongst government regarding how the name ought to be spelt. The online digital atlas maintained by the Nova Scotian government[†] spells the name 'Pipers Cove' and this spelling was confirmed in my

---

[*] Transcriptions of Father Pacifique Guide to Micmac Place Names, 1934, pp. 261 via Mi'kmaq Place Names Digital Atlas.

[†] Maintained by the Geographic Information Services (GeoNOVA) unit, part of the Department of Service Nova Scotia and Internal Services within the Nova Scotian government.

correspondence with an officer of the provincial Geographic Names Program.

The origin of the name Pipers Cove can be traced back to an ancestor of early residents of the area who was a talented bagpiper. Decedents of this renowned bagpiper became known as the 'Piper' branch of the Clan MacNeil. These descendants settled the area now known as Pipers Cove and thus the area became known as Pipers Cove as it was where the 'Piper MacNeils' or 'Pipers' lived.

The sterile information provided by the Geographic Information Service's GeoNAMES online atlas notes that Pipers Cove was a locality until being upgraded to a community on 26 June 2007 and that the area was named after Roderick McNeil (sic) who lived in the area and died in 1835. This information is attributed to the postmaster of Pipers Cove in 1922.[*] This explanation only begins to scratch the surface of the rich story behind the name.

Renowned Canadian folklorist Edith Fowke recorded information about the origin of the name in her book *Folklore in Canada*[†]. It notes that the namesake of Pipers Cove allegedly gained his gift for piping after an encounter with a fairy – a common mythical creature in Scottish Gaelic lore – inside a *Sithean* or fairy hill, where the creatures are said to reside. To complicate matters, the 1967 book *Place-Names and Places of Nova Scotia* published by the Public Archives of Nova Scotia provides a more comprehensive history of the name and dates it to back 1825 but attributes it to Norman MacNeil, not Roderick. It says that Norman was piper to the Laird of Barra before

---

[*] It was common for English language place names in Cape Breton to be determined by the postmaster because many communities had only a Gaelic language name until the turn of the twentieth century. Gaelic names were not accepted by the Celtophobic Canadian government at the time.

[†] Fowke, Edith, "The Marvellous Piper" as told by Mrs Dave Patterson, Folklore in Canada, Toronto: MacClelland and Stewart Inc., 1982, pp. 129-130.

coming to Nova Scotia in 1802 and settling at what became known as Pipers Cove in 1803. Those dates would place Norman amongst the original cohort of Barra settlers.

The mystery surrounding the origin of the name does not end there. A. J. MacKenzie's 1926 book, *History of Christmas Island Parish**, provides not only a comprehensive history of the church parish but also of the families in the district. It does not explicitly note a namesake for Pipers Cove but does tell the story of Rory 'Piper' MacNeil and several of his descendants who were the first settlers at what became known as Pipers Cove.

Rory MacNeil is described as a very strong, masculine Barraman known for his great talent in playing the bagpipes. Interestingly, despite a difference in name attributed to the talented piper, MacKenzie also recounts a legend that this talent was acquired in a fairy hill. MacKenzie sets out the genealogy of each family in great detail, and his original 1926 publication is generally accepted by the local community. It is for this reason that I believe the namesake of Pipers Cove was indeed Rory 'Piper' MacNeil, but in rather a roundabout way, for it was his descendants who became known as the 'Piper' branch of the Clan MacNeil because of their ancestor's talent with the bagpipes and it was these descendants that later gave Pipers Cove its name.

Rory MacNeil was born in Barra in Scotland sometime in the late eighteenth century. He was piper to the Laird of Barra, who, coincidentally, had a son named Roderick MacNeil who came to Canada but died on the Plains of Abraham at Quebec in 1759 – well before Scottish settlement in Cape Breton. The following excerpt provides a sense of his great talent and the respect held for him amongst his kith and kin:

---

* A. J. MacKenzie, History of Christmas Island Parish, 1926, pp. 81-83.

(Rory) was descended from famous pipers, but he excelled them all. Tradition has it that he was the best piper in Scotland in his days, and that it was in a fairy hill (sitein) [sic] that he received his great musical gifts. There is another tradition amongst his descendants to the effect that on one occasion it was his great strength, his power of endurance and his ability to make the bagpipes sound loud and far that saved many lives from perishing from hunger and cold on a bleak islet on the mainland coast [of Scotland].*

The story then goes on to explain that the Laird of Barra and the Laird MacDonald, along with a large entourage, were returning to the Hebrides by ship after being away when they were driven off course by a terrible storm and wrecked on an island off the coast of Scotland, which was then enveloped by a thick fog that prevented their getting under way again. Many of those stranded began to lose hope as they had no food, but Rory MacNeil, having a pair of bagpipes, played a tune that communicated the player was experiencing duress. He played so loudly that it was heard on the mainland and a rescue party soon came to the aid of those stranded. The Laird MacNeil took Rory's son, John, into his employment as a token of appreciation to Rory for saving him and the rest of those who had been stranded.

This son, John, married and had seven sons: Hector, Rory (Jr), Malcolm, Donald, Neil, Angus, and Allan. Being descendants of Rory 'Piper', they were known throughout the community as being 'Pipers' because of their talented grandfather. John's sons Hector and Rory (Jr) were two of the 370 Barramen who arrived at Pictou in 1802 and in 1803 they both travelled to Pipers Cove to stake out land for future settlement.

It was in 1805 that Hector MacNeil settled at Pipers Cove. His son Malcolm, who was born on the day that Hector and

---

* A. J. MacKenzie, History of Christmas Island Parish, 1926, pp. 81-82.

his wife, Sarah, arrived at Pipers Cove, later built the first frame house in the district. The inspiration for this new style of dwelling came during a visit to Sydney for supplies. Malcolm saw a man putting up a frame house – there were only log cabins in the Grand Narrows district until that time – and he commenced constructing a similar frame house for himself upon his return to Pipers Cove.

It is not clear that Rory 'Piper' MacNeil ever left Scotland, but it is clear that the community was named after the MacNeils who settled the area, who were denoted by their nickname as the 'pipers', and therefore the name is indirectly attributable back to Rory 'Piper' MacNeil. He gave this branch of Clan MacNeil the 'pipers' moniker from which the name Pipers Cove is derived.

Also of note from A. J. MacKenzie's *History of Christmas Island Parish*[*] is the use of the spelling 'Darby's Point' rather than Derby Point. Unfortunately, no detail is given as to the origin of this name in the book, nor is any explanation of the name provided in the Geographic Information Service's GeoNAMES online atlas, although it appears the decision to officially affirm the name Derby Point occurred in 1950.

The owner of the Old Glebe House before its acquisition by the Ramsay family was responsible for moving the house to its present location in the early twentieth century. The late Dan B. MacNeil was born in 1883, the same year that the third church was constructed. Dan B. MacNeil married the late Mary Ann MacNeil, his third cousin.[†] Dan B. MacNeil was the son of Michael D. MacNeil (1843-1926) and Catherine (Katie) MacNeil (1848-1942). Katie was the daughter of John and Peggie Currie of Big Pond. Michael

---

[*] A. J. MacKenzie, History of Christmas Island Parish, 1926, pp. 84.

[†] MacLean, Basil, MacNeil Family Tree, pp. 3, published online at the Clan MacLean Atlantic Branch website, see www.clanmacleanatlantic.org/gen/basilmacnlean_AT_yahoo_DOT_ca.pdf, accessed 14 October 2021.

D. MacNeil was himself the son of Donald MacNeil (1802-1866) and Margaret MacNeil* (1806-unknown). Donald was the son of Hector and Sarah MacNeil (nee MacInnis), the same Hector who was one of the first settlers at Pipers Cove. As previously recounted, Hector MacNeil was the son of John MacNeil, who was himself the son of the famed Rory (Piper) MacNeil, who allegedly gained his gift for piping in a fairy hill; Dan B. MacNeil was therefore descended from the 'Piper MacNeils', who gave Pipers Cove its name.

OPPOSITE PAGE Excerpt showing the Grand Narrows District from the A. F. Church *Map of Cape Breton County,* circa 1879. Each house is annotated with the name of the head of the household. Note 'Mrs McNeil' is listed as the head of the household of the propety that would later become Derbywood. MAP IN PUBLIC DOMAIN

---

* Other sources state that Donald's wife's name was Mary. The author has chosen to use that listed in the family tree by Basil MacLean because he is a relative of Mrs MacNeil and the relationship of the author of the dissenting source is unknown. Thus, Mr MacLean is considered the source most likely to be correct. Refer to MacLean, Basil, MacNeil Family Tree, pp. 3, published online at the Clan MacLean Atlantic Branch website, see www.clanmacleanatlantic.org/gen/basilmacnlean_AT_yahoo_DOT_ca.pdf, accessed 14 October 2021.

Landg[?]
Rev M. McKe[?] R.C.
Sch[?]
B.S.
Neilban Cove

STRAITS OF BARRA

N. McNeil Cath[?]
R. McNeil
H. McNeil   D. McNeil
A. McNeil
Fraight H?   A. McNeil
    Store   J. McNeil
        Mrs McNeil
    Mrs R.   J. McDonald
        McNeil

        A. Campbell
                        530

    D. McDonald
        N. McNeil   J. McNeil
        N. McLean   Mrs McNeil
        N. McNeil   P. McNeil
                        Mrs McNeil
by Pt
    M. McNeil
    J. McDonald
        Mrs McDonald
    "That House"   H. McDonald
                                Pt

Folk Beliefs and Lore

The history of the house is intertwined with the history of Scottish Gaels in the district. Despite their Catholic faith, Gaels held many superstitions and folk beliefs that, on the face of it, are not easily reconcilable with strict Latin doctrine. One superstition brought to Nova Scotia by the Gaels was a belief in the so-called 'second sight'. The core of this superstition is that some people can see into the future and can describe events before they take place. This gift of second sight was not something one desired, and it was often considered a burden to the person who possessed it as the events foreseen were often unpleasant such as disasters, deaths, or injuries.[*] It is notable that a resident of the neighbouring community of Benacadie, who allegedly possessed the second sight, sought a cure for this affliction because it caused him enormous grief and trauma. The second sight involved the burdened person having brief visions of events that would later come to be true, such as seeing a mourning party standing around a deceased person in a coffin and happening upon this exact scene in the exact same spot sometime later.

---

[*] Giseagan / Folk Beliefs, Nova Scotia Museum, 2021, accessed 14 October 2021 (see Nova Scotia Museum website > Resources > The Gaels > Giseagan / Folk Beliefs).

Similarly, the Gaels' belief in 'forerunners' were omens of an approaching event, usually bad. Often coming in the form of strange lights, especially when foreshadowing a death, one forerunner appeared as a light hovering over Antigonish Harbour night after night until the body of a drowned boy was found in the same spot that the light had been occurring, after which the light ceased to appear again.[*]

Perhaps the best known of the Gaels' folk beliefs is that of *na sthichean* or the fairies. Unlike Tinkerbell from the well-known Walt Disney picture *Peter Pan*, traditional fairies of Celtic lore are neither friendly nor benign. Rather, these creatures are wingless, ugly, and occasionally dangerous. Sightings and encounters with fairies in Cape Breton date back prior to Scottish settlement. The indigenous Mi'kmaq people share a belief in fairies or 'little people' with the Gaels, despite each culture having originated on opposite sides of the Atlantic. The fairies have not gone away with the passage of time. In fact, records of encounters between locals and mythological creatures such as fairies in the district exist from as late as the year 2000. In the documentary film *The Fairy Faith*[†], several people from central Cape Breton, including both those descended from Scottish Gaels and the indigenous Mi'kmaq people, recount contemporary experiences with the 'little people', as they refer to them.

One encounter, described first-hand by the two young men who experienced it, tells of the time in the late 1990s when they saw a fairy at Pipers Cove. The two young men had swam out from Pipers Cove beach to dive for cohogs along the western cliffs of the cove, past where the old

---

[*] Giseagan / Folk Beliefs, Nova Scotia Museum, 2021, accessed 14 October 2021 (see Nova Scotia Museum website > Resources > The Gaels > Giseagan / Folk Beliefs).

[†] The Fairy Faith, National Film Board of Canada and John Walker Productions Limited, 2000, (From 1 hour 6 minutes through 1 hour 18-minute portion of film).

government wharf once stood. The young men were diving down to the shallow, sandy bottom of the lake together in search of the shellfish. After several dives, the pair surfaced to find a small, humanoid creature looking back at them from the top of the cliff. The location where the creature stood was at the top of the cliffs, adjacent to the upper field at Pipers Cove on the eastern slope of Briomachoal, near where an outcrop of rocks forms a small island. One of the young men noticed the creature first before tapping on his mate's should, who then looked up and saw the creature himself. After observing the creature for a few moments and unsure of what to do, the young men proceeded to continue with their cohog gathering and dove down to the bottom once again. When they surfaced, the creature had disappeared.

Another more sinister local encounter took place at the swimming hole just north of the small wooden bridge in Benacadie Glen Road. The bridge is located just east of the crossroads of Castle Bay Road, Woods Road, Farrell Settlement Road, and Benacadie Glen Road in Rear Christmas Island. The swimming hole is accessible by a rudimentary path leading from the road. This encounter left those who experienced it with a fear so deep that they refused to return to the site, although prior to the encounter the spot had been a favourite picnic spot for the family involved. Two of the women who experienced the encounter had not returned to the site for a quarter of a century and only did so reluctantly after being persuaded by documentary filmmakers to recount their experience on-site. In or around 1975, a mother and her children were at the swimming hole picnicking and swimming when suddenly the family heard strange music. It 'sounded like either voices or some kind of instrument. It was just indescribable,'[*] recalled the mother[†]. The music was not gentle nor calming but rather instilled a fear deep within the

---

[*] The Fairy Faith, National Film Board of Canada and John Walker Productions Limited, 2000, 1 hour 14 minutes.

[†] Names have not been used for the privacy of those involved.

mother, who says she panicked and rushed towards the water to retrieve her youngest child who was swimming. She told the other children that they were leaving. The mother became more frightened as the music continued and she asked her daughter, the oldest child present, whether she could also hear the strange music. The daughter responded in the affirmative, which further elevated the mother's fear. She knew that it was real – not a figment of her imagination. She took her younger children and put them inside the car, and yelled after her daughters, who were both older, to hurry and get into the car as quickly as possible. The mother stood outside the car until all the children were safely inside, and then hurriedly alighted herself. As her now-adult daughter recalls, 'it took her a couple of minutes to get into the car, and finally when she got into the car (my mother) told me, "don't look back, don't look back."...I didn't listen to my mom and I got up and I snuck a peek and over there (in the path leading from the swimming hole to the road), I saw one coming out of the woods.' The daughter goes on to explain that this fairy joined a group that had already emerged from the woods. The creatures formed a circle and danced whilst holding hands. Seeing this, the daughter turned back around, sat down in her seat, and tried to forget what she had just witnessed. She later heard legends that if a witness of a fairy sighting told anyone else about their encounter, it would bring bad luck. She did not speak about what she saw with anyone for many years until the mother and daughter pair finally broached the subject in late 1999, when taking part in a documentary film after the filmmaker happened upon their story. The terrorised family would not return to this favourite spot for a quarter of a century. The pair noted that even when they returned in 2000 to be interviewed for the film, they felt as though the creatures were watching them.

Whilst the culture and language at Derbywood ceased to be Gaelic after the acquisition of the property by W. L. Ramsay in 1962, these tales of relatively recent encounters indicate that the Celtic culture continues to live on in the surrounding community. Given the former owner of the property, Mr Dan B. MacNeil, spoke Gaelic as his mother tongue, we can say with reasonable confidence that Celtic tales and folk beliefs would have echoed throughout the house both during his time as resident of the dwelling and further back when it was occupied by the Gaelic priests of St Barra Parish. There is documentary evidence that such superstitions were still relatively widely held as late as 1921, as recorded by Charles W. Dunn in his widely acclaimed book *Highland Settler,* in which a religious gentleman commented:

Perhaps the only bad traits that [the Gaels] brought with them to Cape Breton were their superstitions regarding witches, fairies, ghosts, etc. and their fondness for whisky.[*]

And it was not only Gaelic folk beliefs and superstitions that would have been passed down from generation to generation, prior to the arrival of the ethnically and culturally Anglo-Saxon Ramsay family.

An unexpected and disturbing event took place whilst the house was still located at Christmas Island: the possession of Sarah Catherine MacKenzie, which began in December 1907.[†] A mere two days after J. A. K. Gillis became parish priest at St Barra, a set of strange events centred on nine-year-old Sara took place in the MacKenzie home. Sarah and her sister Mary Elizabeth[‡] – who shared a bedroom or were sharing a bedroom on this particular night – had gone to bed for the evening. No sooner had they gotten into bed when a

---

[*] Dunn, Charles W., Highland Settler, Toronto, University of Toronto Press, 1953, pp. 37 via MacKenzie, Heather Marie, The Historical Development of Christmas Island Parish, 1977, pp. 46 and 66.

[†] MacKenzie, Heather Marie, The Historical Development of Christmas Island Parish, 1977, pp. 47-51. This tale was related to Ms MacKenzie in 1977 by Archie A. MacKenzie but was first recorded by his brother Hugh MacKenzie. The subject of the tale, Sarah Catherine MacKenzie, was the sister of both men.

[‡] Mary later became Sister Carlotta of the Dominicans Order of New York.

loud rapping sound began under Sarah's head. The sound was heard by Mr and Mrs MacKenzie who were in an adjacent room and, alarmed at what was a very unusual sound, went to the girls' room to investigate. It rapidly became apparent that the sound was not of the natural world and holy water, being readily at hand in this devout Catholic household, was sprinkled onto the spot from which the sound was emanating. This caused the sound to become louder and increase in pace. Sarah was at this point removed from the bed to the timber floor, but the rapping sound continued. The family, becoming desperate and increasingly alarmed, began to recite the rosary, with the phrase 'have mercy on us' eliciting an even louder rapping.

The next morning, noting that there were no telephones in the district in 1907, Mr MacKenzie called in to see the newly arrived Father Gillis after Mass. The priest advised the distraught father to call again later that night. The reverend was duly collected and brought to the MacKenzie residence. He blessed the house inside and out in the Latin tradition, and then Sarah was put to bed. The rapping sound returned instantly the moment she laid down. The priest began praying, occasionally sprinkling holy water. The rapping sound continued despite the priest's efforts. Hugh, brother of Sarah, later recalled that Father Gillis said, 'if that was the devil, I'd drive him out quick, but it must be some poor neglected soul who is looking for help.'

The priest advised to continue with the prayers through the night and was confident the sound would cease. The next night, Sarah was moved to what one presumes was the 'sick room', a small bedroom off the parlour common in nineteenth century homes. The rapping began again, and Mr MacKenzie went into the bedroom and was taken aback by what he saw: a ghostly white hand rapping at young Sarah's own hand. Father Gillis was sent for, and he also witnessed the apparition upon entering the bedroom. 'Sure enough, I saw that beautiful hand. It must be an angel for I never saw a hand like it,' the priest was reported to have said afterwards. The ghostly experience continued for some time and neighbours would call in each evening to hear and, occasionally, see the poltergeist.

The rapping continued for about a week, and then one evening Sarah went into a trance and began speaking with people who had died long before she was born. A detailed conversation was purportedly had with the wife of a granduncle. When the trance appeared to be coming to an end, Sarah suffered terribly, and it was feared for a moment she might choke to death. When the trance had ended, Sarah spoke of a ring that this grandaunt had told her about and, when the family looked in the corner of an old trunk upstairs upon Sarah's instructions, the ring in question was discovered despite no one having previously known about it. The trances continued to occur regularly for some time.

Once whilst in a trance, Sarah noted that James MacLean had just died, and she could see him entering purgatory. Startled at this revelation, Mr MacKenzie checked the time and noted it was twenty minutes to eight in the evening. News later arrived with a neighbour at eleven o'clock that night that James MacLean had indeed passed away. When Mr MacKenzie enquired about the time of death, the neighbour responded that he had died about twenty minutes to eight earlier that evening.

Sarah was eventually sent to live in the Glebe House with Father Gillis for a few months so that he could more closely watch over her and the incidents that she was experiencing. She continued to attend school and it is not clear whether any re-occurrence of the rapping or trances took place during her stay at the Glebe House, but her brother Hugh recalled that many priests called into Christmas Island to visit with her and learn about her incredible experiences. When the girl finally returned to live at home, Father Gillis advised the family not to mention the incidents to the girl and it was allegedly never spoken about again.

This peculiar episode took place in late 1907 and early 1908, by which time the parish priest would have been living in the third, Victorian-style glebe house that was constructed in 1896. The third glebe house had replaced the glebe house now located at Derbywood, which was in use from about 1824 through to 1896. No recorded demonic possession took place in the glebe house now at Derbywood, though it is noted that in 1907 it would have been only eleven years since the second (1824) glebe house was superseded and that the Derbywood glebe house was still located in Christmas Island, only a short distance from the new glebe house where the possessed Sarah was staying with Father Gillis.

OPPOSITE PAGE Excerpt showing Christmas Island from the A. F. Church *Map of Cape Breton County,* circa 1879. Each house is annotated with the name of the head of the household. Note 'Rev. M. McKenzie' is listed as the parish priest ('P.P.') at St Barra Church ('R. C. Chapel'). The priest was still living in the Old Glebe House in 1879, thus this map shows the location of the Old Glebe House prior to it being moved to Pipers Cove by Dan B. MacNeil.
MAP IN PUBLIC DOMAIN

Goose Pond

Christmas Id

Steam Boat
Landing
Rev M. McKe... R.C.Chapel
School H^s P.P. A. McNeil A. Gillis
B.S.Sh... D. McNeil A. McKinnon H. McNe...
... Cove J. McKinnon J. Gillis
J. McNeil
R. McNeil
P. McKinnon
Cath. Cemetery J. McKinnon

Store & P.O.
M. McDoug...
M. McDou...
J. McKinnon
J. McDo...

J. Mc...
H. M. N...
H. Mc...

N. McNeil
R. McNeil
D. McNeil
H. McNeil
A. McNeil
A. McNeil
J. McNeil
rs McNeil
McDonald
...Neil

500

530

J. Gillis
R. H. McNeil
M. M. McNeil
S. M...
School
J. McN...

The Hunt for Briomachoal

In the course of researching this book, I came across numerous references to 'Briomachoal' on official government maps. These maps indicated that the hill due east of Derbywood, and on the slopes of which Derbywood sits, is officially named Briomachoal. The name was only used on some official maps and not on others. It was also listed as a 'former official name' in the Nova Scotia GeoNAMES online atlas, yet maps from the 1980s through to the 2000s continued to use the name on occasion, including both provincial and federal maps.

The author enquired with the government department responsible for geographic names in Nova Scotia and a year long search into this name and its status ensued. It was not until I made an enquiry in August 2021 that the name came to the attention of the Geographic Names Program. With the help of a geographic names specialist with the provincial Geographic Names Program, the story of the name Briomachoal was painstakingly uncovered.

The geographic names specialist investigated in her organisation's archives and made enquiries with Gaelic language experts and Gaelic community members to try to ascertain if Briomachoal is indeed a Gaelic word and, if so, if it is spelt correctly. The files in the Geographic Names Program office did not indicate the meaning of the name, but a 1976 set of meeting minutes state that the name is of Gaelic origin and that the meaning and correct spelling are unknown.

Briomachoal does not seem to have appeared on any maps until the 1970s when it was recorded on a mylar field sheet overlay during field research conducted by the Nova Scotian government. The name was subsequently included in a list of recommendations dated 15 December 1975 from the Nova Scotia director of surveys to the Canadian Permanent Committee on Geographic Names. It appears that the name was collected during field interviews with local residents undertaken during the course of the provincial government's field research on geographic names in 1973. Other names included on the same mylar field sheet overlay include Coopers Pond, Kelly Pond, and Rory Charlies Mountain, which have all subsequently become formal place names.

The national committee appears to have deferred a final decision on Bromachoal at its 23 February 1976 meeting, whilst the names Rory Charlies Mountain, Rear Estmere, and Cains Mountain are listed as adopted names. A list of interviews includes M. MacNeil of Pipers Cove. The minutes of the meeting state: *'Briomachoal (This is a gaelic [sic] name for this peak. However, the correct spelling may not be as shown, and its meaning is not known – suggest retain on records until more information becomes available.)'*.

It appears the hill was known as Briomachoal amongst the early Gaelic residents of the area. A handwritten index card from the archive of the Geographic Names Program gives a description as: 'Briomachoal (C. B.), a high round-based, steep-sided hill at Pipers Cove.'

Throughout the post-war period, the provincial government undertook surveys to gather the names of various geographic features across the province. In 1973, a surveyor with the Department of Lands and Forests – the department responsible for geographic names in the province at that time – conducted field research in the Barra Strait area. The surveyor collected the name Briomachoal for the hill between Derbywood and Pipers Cove Beach. The Geographic Names Program archive contains field notes that include a map with a mylar overlay showing Briomachoal handwritten at this location. The field surveyor also undertook interviews with residents of the area to gather as much information about the name as possible.

Briomachoal was included on a 15 December 1975 list of provincial name recommendations to the Permanent Canadian Committee on Geographic Names, the federal body charged with formal approval of geographic names in Canada. The entry in the recommendation list reads 'Briomachoal (Mountain), N. of Bras d'Or L., Cape Breton Co., 45 56 60 46'.

A record of the 23 February 1976 meeting of the Permanent Canadian Committee on Geographic Names includes a minute stating that the decision of the committee was deferred until further research into the correct Gaelic spelling of Briomachoal could take place, with the status of the name set to 'C2 pending'; meaning neither approved nor disapproved. A note alongside the archival record states that it is likely that the initial surveyor spelt the name phonetically when interviewing locals in 1973, as the spelling 'Briomachoal' does not accord with Gaelic spelling conventions.

The archival documents then show that the name was subsequently approved four years later at the 11 February 1980 meeting of the Permanent Canadian Committee on Geographic Names. A handwritten note dated 31 January 1980 is found alongside the formal meeting minutes stating, '[It was] asked if a decision had been made on this name. It was 'pending investigation' on the decision of 23

February 1976. [It was] checked [...] out locally and [reported that] the name was suitable for approval.' A fortnight after approval of the name, the executive secretary for geographic names in Canada wrote to the Nova Scotia Department of Lands and Forests expressing concern about the approval of a single-word name; that is, without a generic term indicating the type of feature the name describes. The 25 February 1980 letter reads:

On February 11 you approved the name Briomachoal. I am concerned about the approval of names without any indication of the generic characteristics of the feature being named. Sometimes terms are quite obscure, such as 'beinn' in Beinn Breagh. Sometimes there are no generics at all, such as Hen and Chickens, with the reader of a map having to draw his own conclusions about the characteristics of the feature or features being named...None of these, however, are exactly the same as adopting a single word for a physical feature, such as the name Briomachoal.

Another uncertainty about Briomachoal is its real Gaelic spelling. Perhaps it should be something like Braigh na Ceal, or a similar name with the Bhreagh of Beinn Bhreagh in the name. Is it better to have a corrupted form of a name than no name at all? I think it would be, since you may never find out the exact spelling of the name.

It would have been preferable in this instance to have adopted Briomachoal Mountain for the feature near Grand Narrows.

A file note dated 13 May 1980 appears to clear up the issue, stating, 'Briomachoal, Gaelic – known to people – just plain Briomachoal – leave decision as is – will write later.' From this we can surmise that investigations into the form of the name were made and the result was that the name, as known and accepted within the community, is Briomachoal, not Briomachoal Mountain.

Briomachoal then appeared on federal and provincial government maps, including the 1981 11-F-15 3rd edition map from the Government of Canada and a 1986 map from the provincial Department of Natural Resources.

In 1988 geographic names were computerised and consolidated into a single digital database. It appears that when Briomachoal was computerised, the 1976 'pending' decision was recorded but the 1980 decision to approve the name was not. A file note also indicates that no record could be found between 1982 and 1988 indicating the name had been rescinded or the status changed back to 'pending'. No paper trail exists to explain why the 1980 decision (and the name) were not incorporated into the new computerised database during the changeover to computer records in 1988. Federal maps between 1988 and 1994, which were based on the new computerised database, removed the name, but a 2003 map created by the provincial Department of Natural Resources included the name.

This is entirely conjecture, but I believe that it is likely an error occurred during computerisation in 1988, which resulted in the name being removed from maps.

The geographic names specialist made enquiries with three Gaelic experts in Nova Scotia to ascertain what the correct Gaelic spelling of Briomachoal ought to be. She received feedback that the name appeared to be Gaelic in origin but was not recognisable. The experts hypothesised a number of meanings and spelling. One theory was that Briomachoal was a corruption of *Braighe MacDhomhnuill* (MacDonald's Hill or MacDonald's Rise; literally 'high land of MacDonald').

It was thought it may perhaps have originated from *Braigh a' chaoil*, meaning 'the high ground / upland / brae of the narrow.' It was noted that this does not match the topography as the hill overlooks a broad, open stretch of Bras d'Or Lake, not the narrows. One expert wrote that a Mr Shamus Y. MacDonald, who has studied central Cape

Breton Gaelic place names extensively, was told by a third party that an old resident of the area used to say that the name was 'an old country name'; that is, from Scotland. This explanation resolves the topography issue as the name would have related to the topography of the original 'Briomachoal' in Scotland, having been transplanted to Cape Breton in a similar manner to the way Inverness and Iona are transplanted names from Scotland. None of the Gaelic experts could find a *Briomachoal* in Scotland, which suggests that the spelling is highly corrupted, if this is the origin of the name. There was no clear or straight forward answer from the Gaelic experts, but they all agreed that the spelling must have diverged significantly because the word does not follow conventional Gaelic spelling.

The geographic names specialist then began internal discussions with her superior at the Geographic Names Program to determine the way forward. At first, the records seemed to indicate that the pending status was possibly an error resulting from the computerisation of records in the 1980s. It appeared it might be possible to simply correct the error and put Briomachoal quite literally back on the map. After further internal discussions and research – and several months – it became clear that the error was not as simple as it first appeared. It is extraordinary to think that the name remained forgotten in limbo for close to thirty-five years until the author stumbled upon the name whilst undertaking research for this book.

It took from August 2021, when I made the first enquiry to the Geographic Names Program, until April 2022 for the way forward to be decided. The original decisions were made by people who are no longer around, and the decision was recorded using methods that are no longer employed: in 1976, paperwork was still being typed up on typewriters and filed in physical filing cabinets and archives. In 2021, the decision-making process and the record keeping methods are entirely computerised and have gone through several iterations of computerisation since the process to covert to digital records began in the 1980s. It is therefore unsurprising that it took the better part of eight months to understand the process that occurred nearly half a century ago and the subsequent record trail from that time to the present.

In April 2022, the geographic names specialist contacted me to confirm that she and her superior had determined that the correct path forward is the lodgement of a formal geographic name change application sponsored by her organisation. This will allow a formal assessment of the name Briomachoal to be undertaken, including field research and community consultation. This process will determine if the name is actually applicable to the hill in question, what the correct spelling ought to be, and what the origin of the name is. It will then allow for a formal recommendation to be made to the relevant authority in government to either make the name official or to rescind the name. In either instance, at the end of the process, the limbo status of Briomachoal will be resolved after nearly half a century. If all goes well, we may see the name return to maps – and mapping programs on our computers and mobile phones – in the future.

Every Coin in the Coffer that Rings

The built form* of the Old Glebe House suggests its history, beginning as a relatively modest residence for the local Roman Catholic priest and then being used as the homestead for a working farm in the early to mid-twentieth century, before becoming a summer retreat for a large, middle class, late twentieth century suburban family.

Until W. L. Ramsay purchased the estate now known as Derbywood in 1962, the property was a working farm. When the previous owner died, his widow sold the house

---

* For a complete assessment of the built form and vernacular architecture of the house, see 'Mader, Mitchell, The Old Glebe House: An examination of the history, social function, and architectural features of the Old Glebe House at Derbywood Estate, Piper's Cove, Nova Scotia, 2012,' available at the Beaton Institute, Cape Breton University, Sydney, Nova Scotia (record number PAM 4060). This paper includes history and assessment of the built form, but some historical facts have been dis-proven whilst researching this book. This book should be taken to be correct where facts diverge between the two. Known mistakes in the 2012 paper include the location of the Pipers Cove school and a statement about the kitchen table in the Old Glebe House having been built especially for the house; in fact, the table was built to suit the size of the Ramsay family but was originally used at the family's primary residence at Sydney River. It was custom built for the family, not the house.

and its contents to W. L. Ramsay and went to live with her sister in MacKinnon's Harbour, and the late Mr MacNeil was waked in the house, with the coffin placed in the parlour.* The house was left untouched when it was sold to Mr Ramsay. Dishes were still on the table and almost all the contents of the house came with it. It is described as if Mrs MacNeil simply stood up, walked out, and never returned. Mrs MacNeil apparently packed only a suitcase before departing to live with her sister. Mr Ramsay dumped multiple loads of unwanted household goods when he took possession of the house in 1962.†

An ancient artefact that came with the house and which remains in possession of the Ramsay family is a Roman Catholic shadow box depicting the crucifixion of Christ. Entitled *Thy Kingdom Come*, the box dates from 1877 and was one of many produced to celebrate the 50th anniversary of the ordination of Pope Pius IX as a bishop. Pius IX was pope from 1846 through 1878 and is best remembered for permanently losing control of the once vast Papal States, bringing about the modern Vatican City microstate.

After losing control of the Roman Catholic church's empire to the Kingdom of Italy in 1870, he refused to leave Vatican City as a form of protest and referred to himself as a 'prisoner of the Vatican'. The loss of the Papal States resulted in the transformation of the Roman Catholic Church from an organisation focussed on governing its empire to one focussed on the spiritual welfare of its followers. It is the reason that the Church retains sovereignty today; Vatican City is a remnant of the former Papal States, a country that once dominated central Europe.

---

* As told to me by a woman working as a costumed interpreter at Baile nan Gàidheal (Highland Village) in the mid to late 2000s. She claimed to be a distant relative of the widow of Dan B. MacNeil. She claimed to have been at Mr MacNeil's wake inside the house in 1962.

† This was a common practice at the time prior to municipal hard rubbish collections.

Pius IX's reign is the longest *verified* reign of any pope on record. Although initially viewed as a progressive, much of his reign was marked by conservative pronouncements and attempts to exert control over Catholics – and wider society – to stem the tide of liberalism, modernism, moral relativism, secularisation, and separation between the church and state. His legacy is not one that would be celebrated by modern standards in which secularisation, separation of church and state, and equality of all are widely held and cherished values.

The shadow box dates from 1877, when the Old Glebe House was still in use as the parish priest's residence at St Barra Parish in Christmas Island. Whilst no records exist to confirm that the shadow box came from the house's time as a glebe house, it is the most likely origin. The box was not purely decorative; the purchaser was not only buying a wall decoration but also a spiritual coupon for 100 fewer days spent in purgatory when they died, or, in the capitalist spirit of the Roman Catholic Church, these 100 days could be 'cashed in' and applied to a recently deceased relative through one's local parish priest.

Called 'indulgences', the Roman Catholic church operated a large scale 'sin forgiving' industry throughout the world and is the source of the old Protestant saying, 'for every coin in the coffer that rings, a soul from purgatory springs.' It was the sale of indulgences that helped spark the Protestant Reformation, in which people across northern Europe began to reject their Papal overlords and seek spiritual salvation directly with God, in essence cutting out the 'middleman' – and his fees. The book *History of the Christian Church* summarises the issue of indulgences succinctly:

Nowhere, except in the lives of the popes themselves, did the humiliation of the Western Church find more conspicuous exhibition than in the sale of indulgences. The forgiveness of sins was bought for money, and this sacred privilege formed the occasion of the rupture of Western

*Christendom as, later, the Lord's Supper became the occasion of the chief division between the Protestant Churches.**

The theory behind indulgences is essentially that firstly, the Roman Catholic Church views itself as the only true church and thus has access to an unlimited 'reserve' of Christian merit, which it can use to 'top up' the moral and spiritual merit of individuals who have committed sins. A good analogy is to view entry to heaven as requiring a ticket, and that ticket is paid for in merit that one accumulates over a lifetime. Good deeds and obedience increase merit and sins decrease merit, much the same way as deposits and withdrawals increase and decrease a bank account. When you die, you can only go straight to heaven if you have enough merit to 'pay' for your entry ticket, otherwise you are sent to purgatory to wait whilst you build up additional merit. However, the Roman Catholic Church has an unlimited reserve of merit and can top up the 'merit balance' of living or deceased individuals and gladly did so – for a fee. The Church developed a system of selling and buying heavenly merit that is not altogether different from modern carbon trading schemes.

The shadow box contains an inscription reading 'Thy Kingdom Come, 100 days indulgence each time (Pius IX, 14th June, 1877)'. It was customary to receive a physical object, called indulgence articles, in return for purchasing an indulgence from the Holy See in Rome, which had to be purchased through a sophisticated sales network in which each 'middleman' got a cut of the profits. Usually, a small crucifix in a bottle was provided to the purchaser, but during the special Golden Jubilee of Pius IX becoming a bishop, these more elaborate indulgence articles were distributed. A document produced by the International Crusade for Holy Relics USA discusses the 1877 Pius IX

---

* Schaff, Philip, History of the Christian Church, volume 6, 'The Middle Ages: From Boniface VIII., 1294 to the Protestant Reformation, 1517, section 80, 1910.

shadow boxes: 'It is described as a "framed crucifix", with metal ornaments symbolic of various aspects of Jesus' life and resurrection. The background is a print of Jerusalem, and there is a card at the bottom that reads "Thy Kingdom Come, 100 days indulgence each time, Pius IX, 14th June 1877".'

There is a long-held belief that the shadow box at the Old Glebe House was one of only eight in existence. Baile nan Gàidheal (Highland Village) Museum also has one in their collection. It is far more likely that, if this story holds any truth at all, the box is one of only eight in existence *in Cape Breton*. An Internet search abounds with duplicate boxes for sale, often selling for between US$100 and US$300.

Incription inside the shadow box reading 'Thy Kingdom Come, 100 Days Indulgence Each Time (Pius IX, 14th June, 1877).
PHOTOGRAPH COURTESY JEFF RAMSAY

The indulgence article shadow box celebrating the fiftieth anniversary of Pope Pius IX becoming a bishop.
PHOTOGRAPH COURTESY JEFF RAMSAY

From Glebe House to Farm House – by Sleigh

The entry for Pipers Cove in *Place-Names and Places in Nova Scotia* notes that a new schoolhouse was built in Pipers Cove in 1867 but burnt down soon after opening. The entry for Pipers Cove also notes that the 1956 population was 68 residents, describing fishing and farming as the main industries in the locality.

It was originally thought that the location of the school may have been where the circa 1980 'New House' currently stands at Derbywood, as several Ramsay siblings recall the ruins of a foundation at that location prior to the house being constructed. Indeed, the stones from this ruined foundation can still be found in the forested hillside south of the 'New House' on the water side of a large row of trees. Whilst researching this book, the author corresponded with Mr Basil MacLean, a relative of Dan B. MacNeil, who shed light on the true origins of this ruined foundation.

The schoolhouse is shown on A. F. Church's map of Cape Breton County,* as being located on the Pipers Cove side of Derby Point in an area that is no longer inhabited. The

---

* Reflex copy of A. F. Church Map, Cape Breton County, No. E-14-6 (Sheet 2 of 2). Obtained by post from The Natural Sciences Library, Nova Scotia Department of Natural Resources, Halifax, Nova Scotia.

section of Derby Point Road that the schoolhouse was in was replaced by a new road further inland in the 1980s[*] and much of the old road has now been eroded and fallen into the lake. It is likely the precise location of the schoolhouse no longer exists, as it appears to be on the water side of the old Derby Point Road. The school was built in the 1890s. The teacher at the one room schoolhouse was Mr Thomas Pembroke. When the Pipers Cove and Grand Narrows schools were eventually consolidated, the tax rate for the property now known as Derbywood dropped by half.

Dan B. MacNeil purchased the Old Glebe House from St Barra Parish and had the house pulled on large sleds over the snow and ice by a team of horses to its current location at Pipers Cove. He erected several barns, which still existed when the Ramsay family took over the property but have subsequently been demolished.[†] Dan B. MacNeil's mother also lived at the property and it was from his parents that he acquired the property.[‡] Mrs MacNeil, Donald Boniface's mother, lived in a modest home located where the 'New House' currently stands; the ruined foundation remembered by the Ramsay siblings was very likely the foundation for Mrs MacNeil's house – not the old Pipers Cove school as previously postulated.[§]

---

[*] The decade of the road works was confirmed by Jeanne Mader, one of W. L. Ramsay's children, who was a young adult during the 1980s and remembers the works being undertaken to move the road inland.

[†] Much of the fabric of the built form heritage of the Old Glebe House and Derbywood remained intact until the 1980s, when the Ramsay family undertook a systemic modernisation programme that resulted in the destruction of the bulk of the material heritage at the site. The Old Glebe House itself has only remnants of its historical fabric as it has been extensively altered both inside and out.

[‡] According to correspondence between the author and Basil MacLean, a relative of the MacNeil family familiar with the history of the property.

[§] In The Old Glebe House, a paper written in 2012 about the history of the house and on deposit with the Beaton Institute at Cape Breton University, it was claimed that the foundation was for the school. This

The name Derbywood was given to the property by W. L. Ramsay upon his acquisition of the house and land in 1962, when the widow of Dan B. MacNeil sold the property following her husband's death. It is not known whether the property had a name prior to its acquisition by Mr Ramsay, but it is almost certain that any name or moniker that it was known by before 1962 would have been in Gaelic, not English, as census records indicate that Gaelic was the first language of Dan B. MacNeil. Indeed, many residents of the district born before the mid-twentieth century would have spoken Gaelic as their first language, before discriminatory government policies forced the language into retreat.

The story of the Old Glebe House and its move from Christmas Island as told by Mr Basil MacLean is:

The story of the Glebe House [being] purchased [by Dan B. MacNeil] and moved from the original location...is true. There was a document at the present Glebe House which stated this and had the details of it. I have tried to acquire that document from [the] caretaker of the building, but he tells me that the Diocese of Antigonish has taken [all] records from the building and will not release them. So it may still exist, but may not be attainable.*

Mrs Isobel Quinn, who lived across the glen from Derbywood, recounted many times that when she was a child the house was pulled by a team of horses 'across the ice' from Christmas Island to its present location in Pipers Cove after Dan B. MacNeil purchased it from the church.

In the 1990s a man visited Derbywood and asked to walk the grounds. He said that he had grown up at Derbywood but was not the biological child of the MacNeils. Mr

---

has been dis-proven and photographs of Mrs MacNeil's home at the location in question have been acquired by the author.

* Direct quote from correspondence between the author and Mr MacLean.

MacLean was able to shed light on this part of the property's history as well:

There were no natural children from Dan B. and Mary Ann [his wife], and when you do the math from the marriage [certificates] and death [certificates], I think it shows that they were not young when they married. But they did adopt two boys who grew up with them. The boys always knew they were adopted...[*]

Dan B. MacNeil and Mary Ann MacNeil were third cousins; Donald Boniface's paternal grandfather was the brother of Mary Ann's paternal grandfather. Given the small number of settlers in the district in the early years – and the large number of MacNeils in the area – it is not surprising that cousins married cousins, given the limited dating pool, especially before the development of the motorcar allowed for dating further afield.

A story related to me by a local lady, who said she learnt it from her father many years ago, told of an event I have called the 'Battle of Derbywood' – a military exercise gone wrong. The Royal Canadian Navy carried out military drills in Bas d'Or Lake from the 1920s through to the 1950s, including torpedo testing and live ordnance exercises. During one such exercise, in the 1920s or 1930s, a cow owned by Dan B. MacNeil was killed by rogue gunfire whilst grazing in the paddocks at Derbywood. It is unclear whether the cow's death was intentional, but Dan B. MacNeil was apparently quite upset and was eventually compensated for the lost cow by the navy. In 2019, the *Cape Breton Post* revealed that the Canadian Department of National Defence understands there to be both spent and live ordnance in Bras d'Or Lake as a result of the exercises carried out in the mid-twentieth century and that live ordnance could pose a significant risk if it were to wash up or be unearthed as part of works.

---

[*] Direct quote from correspondence between the author and Mr MacLean.

The Old Glebe House as it appears in present day, circa 2020.
PHOTO BY ROCHELLE MACQUEEN

View of Briomachoal (mountain) circa 1902, prior to the Old Glebe House being brought to the property by Dan B. MacNeil. Discovered in a photo book featuring scenes from across Cape Breton published in 1903.
PUBLIC DOMAIN PHOTOGRAPH

View of Derbywood and Briomachoal (mountain), late 1980s.
RAMSAY FAMILY COLLECTION

The 'New House' at Derbywood, constructed circa 1980.
RAMSAY FAMILY COLLECTION

View of Bras D'Or Lake from the 'New House' at Derbywood, late 1980s. RAMSAY FAMILY COLLECTION

View of Briomachoal (mountain) and the beach at Derbywood, late 1980s. RAMSAY FAMILY COLLECTION

The Old Glebe House lifted off the ground, with construction of the new foundation ongoing below during 1985 renovation.
RAMSAY FAMILY COLLECTION

The Old Glebe House during the 1985 renovation.
RAMSAY FAMILY COLLECTION

Recently renovated house with new deck, late 1980s.
RAMSAY FAMILY COLLECTION

The Achitectual Development
of the Dwelling

The house was built as the residence for the local Roman Catholic parish priest and, although heavily altered, the original social functions of the dwelling remain evident in remnant architectural features and the general scale and layout of the building. Built in the 1820s as a replacement for the original rudimentary glebe house of log construction, the built form of the house is indicative of the broader district's development from the time the first settlers landed in the early years of the nineteenth century through to firmly established European settlement at the turn of the twentieth century, when an ornate Victorian mansion was constructed as a replacement glebe house.[*]

The Old Glebe House represented a midway point between rudimentary provisional architecture erected in the first years of European settlement and ornate 'statement' architecture erected after European settlement had been firmly established and settlers had sufficient time and resources to erect buildings that were decorative rather than strictly utilitarian. A log cabin gets the job done whilst a

---

[*] This Victorian mansion was destroyed by fire in 1926 and replaced by a large, much less ornate structure in 1927, which still stands at the site today.

Victorian mansion sends a message of confidence and prosperity.

The Old Glebe House was built with separate parlour and kitchen areas and a sick room was located off the parlour.* Built in the 'centre chimney' house style common amongst early Scottish Nova Scotian settlers, a distinctive feature of the dwelling was the dual fireplaces in the kitchen and parlour that made use of the large central chimney. As common in many Cape Breton homes, the kitchen – not the parlour – was the centre of social activity in the home during its early years. This tradition is carried on by the Ramsay family during the summer months to this day.

Constructed of rough wood, the dwelling contains more ornamental features than would have generally been found in a house erected by and for the average settler. Ornate remnant original trim is found throughout the dwelling. A house very similar in design and vintage was acquired some years ago by Baile nan Gàidheal (Highland Village) Museum in Iona and restored to its original early nineteenth century appearance. The level of decoration in that dwelling – which has a nearly identical floor layout but is slightly smaller – is much less. Given the Old Glebe House was originally constructed as a residence for the local parish priest, it is not surprising that the house was built with more ornate decor given the reverence that devout Roman Catholics of the time displayed for their spiritual leaders, who they viewed as being directly in communication with God.†

At some point, a wood stove was added to the house. This wood stove – of the 'pot belly' style – survived into the early twenty-first century inside the Old Glebe House until it was removed to the outside of the house and the elements

---

* Sick rooms off parlours was a common design feature of houses of this period.

† Roman Catholics believe that a priest is required for communication with God, hence the Catholic traditions of mass and confession.

began to take their toll, all but destroying this historic object. The stove contained ornate decorations that suggest it was from the late Victorian or Edwardian period. The kitchen contains a closed off metal plate indicating where a stove was connected to the chimney. A second vent is evident but has been plastered over. The kitchen also contains a square vent that allowed warm air to rise up to one of the bedrooms at the second storey. This vent was boarded over when new plywood flooring was laid in the bedroom above the kitchen in the late 1990s but is still visible from the kitchen. Until it was boarded over, there was a wooden insert that allowed the vent to be closed off when not in use, ensuring no one accidentally stepped into the vent, which would almost certainly have resulted in an injury of some kind. The vent is roughly one square foot in area.

The defining feature of the house until the mid-1980s was the central stone chimney. The chimney was very large, and the space left after the removal of the chimney was sufficiently spacious to house a lavatory. The chimney had to be removed when the house was renovated because lifting the house off the stumps on which it had been sitting also required lifting the chimney, which subsequently collapsed.

The invoice for the works undertaken to the house provides a trove of information about what was done and when. In the summer of 1985, Norman Bushell House Moving Limited of North Sydney was contracted to raise the house, construct a modern foundation, and undertake associated minor works to the dwelling itself. The invoice lists the customer simply as 'Ramsay' and the address is listed as 'Summer cabin' at Pipers Cove and dated 7 July 1985. The dossier lists the works to be undertaken as raising the house, which measures 26.6 by 33 (presumably feet, but no unit of measurement is given). The chimney was to be removed and a 4.4-foot-high '6 by 18' footer wall dug, poured, and back filled. The wall is specified as being 8 inches thick. Putting the 'door back in the wall' is also specified, along with installing three air vent holes in a wall and a 6 by 6 girder installed under the house. Concrete jack post pads and steel jack posts are also listed as works to be undertaken. Finally, the invoice concludes with the repair or replacement of the sills, tearing off the old porch, and installing a 'drain inside of wall'.

The cost is listed as $5860 in total (approximately $14,586 in 2023 with inflation*), with $2900 paid on commencement of the works, $1900 on 2 August (presumably part way through the works), and the balance of $1060 paid on completion.

Robert 'Robbie' Ramsay, second eldest son of W. L. Ramsay, signed the invoice. The works were organised by the children of W. L. Ramsay, who wanted to fix up the then-160-year-old house for their own use. W. L. Ramsay had built and relocated to the so-called 'New House' a few years earlier, which lies about 100 metres south of the Old Glebe House.

Unfortunately, within a decade of the works being undertaken, the new foundation began to crack, twist, and collapse inward. This has continued to worsen with each year and is likely to require either a new foundation be constructed or the demolition of this historic dwelling altogether within the next few decades as the foundation continues its glacial-paced collapse.

Post-renovation – as well-intentioned as the renovation may have been – the dwelling is a shadow of its former self from a built heritage perspective. The bulk of the heritage both inside and outside of the house was lost in 1985, with plastic vinyl siding nailed over the historic external wooden shingles, the original windows ripped out and replaced with ill-suited 1980s era wooden windows that neither function well nor sit comfortably within the facade, and asphalt shingles plastered over the roof of the house.

---

* Canadian dollars; Bank of Canada inflation calculator.

Donald Boniface 'Dan B.' MacNeil and his wife Mary Ann MacNeil and one of their adopted sons outside of the house standing in front of the porch, which was demolished in 1985.
PHOTOGRAPH COURTESY BASIL MACLEAN

A view of the house from the southeast, with the crumbling 1985 concrete foundation visible. PHOTO BY ROCHELLE MACQUEEN

The upper field adjacent to the house. PHOTO BY ROCHELLE MACQUEEN

The lower field adjacent to the house, showing 'Rhodesian strip road' style driveway. PHOTO BY ROCHELLE MACQUEEN

The post-1985 renovated kitchen with old country sink visible.
PHOTO BY ROCHELLE MACQUEEN

Dining area of kitchen with stairwell protruding from ceiling and wall visible. PHOTO BY ROCHELLE MACQUEEN

Original glass cabinet, filled with antique glass bottles found on the property, surrounded by artefacts that have been passed down with the house including a hand-power clothes wringer.
PHOTO BY ROCHELLE MACQUEEN

A closed-off steel wood stove chimney connection pipe. A second closed-off pipe is visible at the left and has been plastered and painted over. PHOTO BY ROCHELLE MACQUEEN

Now closed-off heat vent that allowed warm air to be drawn up to the upper floor. There was once a wooden plug that allowed the vent to be open and closed as needed. PHOTO BY ROCHELLE MACQUEEN

A view down the stairwell, with original door used to close off access between the ground and upper floor visible.
PHOTO BY ROCHELLE MACQUEEN

A view of the upper floor dormer and stairwell.
PHOTO BY ROCHELLE MACQUEEN

Upper floor corridor looking towards a broom cupboard. The lavatory built in the cavity created by the removal of the chimney is located to the right. PHOTO BY ROCHELLE MACQUEEN

Horse-drawn hay rake, a remnant of the estate's days as a working farm, in the upper field adjacent to the house.
PHOTO BY ROCHELLE MACQUEEN

Historic cupboard in former dining room (now used as a bedroom) on the ground floor. PHOTO BY ROCHELLE MACQUEEN

Peeling aged wallpaper reveals several layers of older wallpaper underneath, dating from the early twentieth century.
PHOTO BY ROCHELLE MACQUEEN

Historical doorknob and machanism. PHOTO BY ROCHELLE MACQUEEN

The former workshop room on the upper floor of the house was renovated and turned into a bedroom in the 1980s.
PHOTO BY ROCHELLE MACQUEEN

Lavatory built in the cavity left by the removal of the enormous stone chimney during 1985 renovation. PHOTO BY ROCHELLE MACQUEEN

Lower staircase and landing, with original bannister viewed from front porch. A remnant disused electric light switch is visible at the right of the landing, which has not worked since the house was rewired.
PHOTO BY ROCHELLE MACQUEEN

Original cupboard in kitchen, which is also partially visible in a photograph of previous owner Dan B. MacNeil and his wife Mary Ann. Entry to the old porch was to the immediate right of this cupboard. PHOTO BY ROCHELLE MACQUEEN

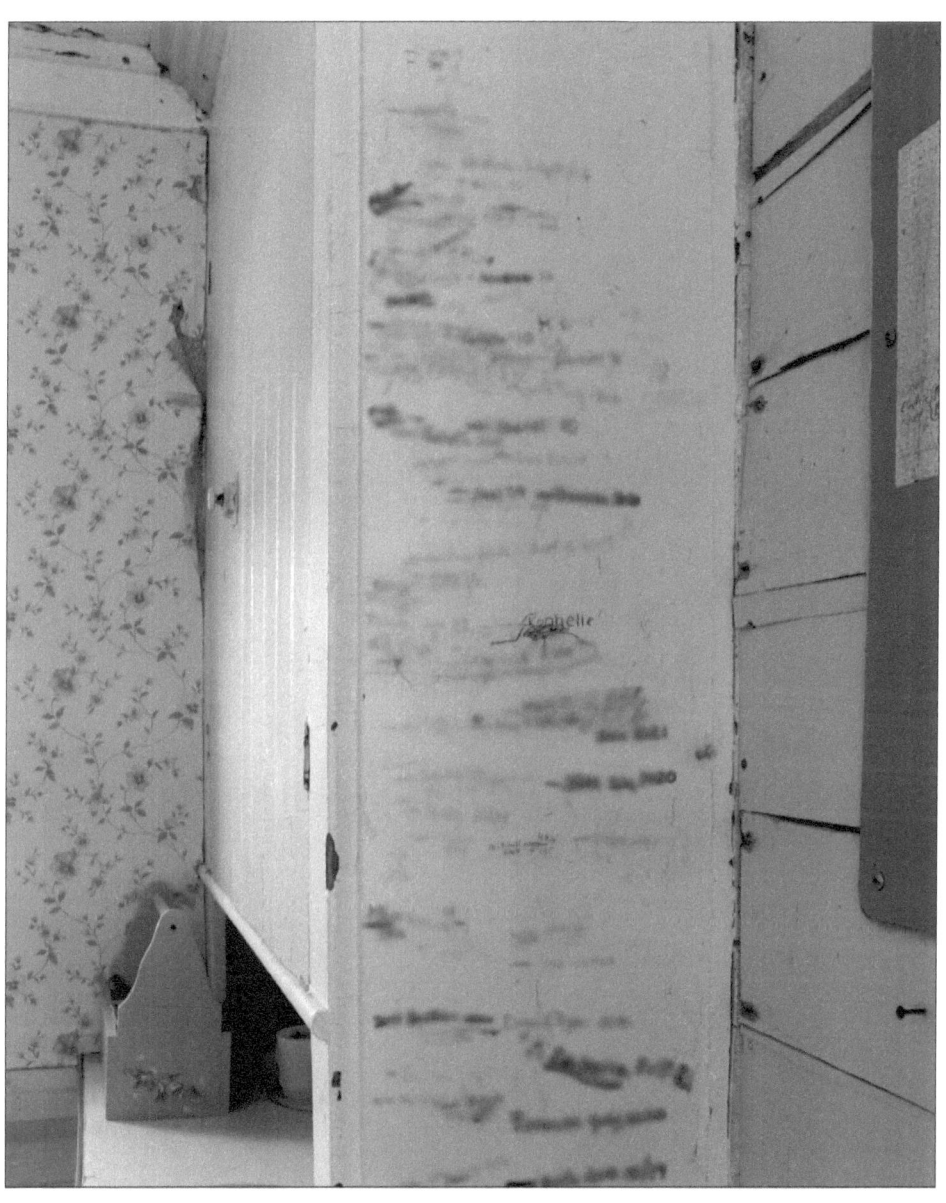

The side of the cupboard has been used as a measuring chart for generations of Ramsay children, inlcuding both contributors to this book. PHOTO BY ROCHELLE MACQUEEN

Antique refrigerators used as 'beer fridges' have been a staple of the house's time being used as a summer home. This model replaced a slightly earlier model. PHOTO BY ROCHELLE MACQUEEN

View of the upper portion of the original staircase, with unusually deep steps by modern standards. PHOTO BY ROCHELLE MACQUEEN

External view of location of former porch, which was removed in the 1985 renovation. PHOTO BY ROCHELLE MACQUEEN

View of passageway created by the removal of the large central chimney during the 1985 renovation. The size of the chimney, which was a defining feature of the house, is evidenced by the size of the space it left behind. The lavatory is located in same space on the upper floor. PHOTO BY ROCHELLE MACQUEEN

Postscript

History does not stand still, but marches relentlessly onwards and I hope that future generations will continue to record the history of the house as it progresses.

Writing this history from such a distance has been a challenge. If it were not for the Internet, it would certainly have required many more trips back to Cape Breton. Notwithstanding the help of the Internet, much of the archival information required physically mailing items across continents from Nova Scotia to Melbourne. The gaps in the story were filled during my 2023 trip to Cape Breton, where I spent many hours in the archives at both the Sydney Library and the Cape Breton University Library. By the time I returned to Melbourne, I could thread a microfilm reader with my eyes closed.

The historical A. F. Church maps, a series of maps of each county in Nova Scotia drawn in the late nineteenth century showing not only every single dwelling, but the name of the head of each household as well, are not yet online and I had to purchase enormous photostats of the Cape Breton and Victoria county maps. The month long wait for them to arrive in the post was extremely tantalising but worth it. Likewise, MacKenzie's master thesis from 1977 on the historical development of Christmas Island parish was only found because I had come across it with the help of Pauline MacLean at the Baile nan Gàidheal (Highland Village) archive in Iona a decade ago. Pauline graciously scanned and sent me an electronic copy as I only had a few excerpt pages from my undergraduate paper that inspired this book.

I had wanted to write this book for a long time, but it was not until the pandemic struck and I suddenly found myself unable to return to Cape Breton that this project took off. It was helpful to have something to work on whilst stuck in my house for the better part of two years. Researching and writing about Cape Breton was cathartic. I felt connected to the old country at a time that I was unable to visit.

It is a shame that the Diocese of Antigonish refuses to discuss the records it has in its archive relating to the history of the house, for I suspect such records would make this story all the richer. At the very least, and in spite of the efforts of the Catholic Church to suppress any stories relating to the former St Barra Parish at Christmas Island, we have confirmation from two separate sources that the house was indeed moved sometime around the turn of the twentieth century. I only wish that the exact date and details of the move were known. Perhaps one day the Church will open their archives and we will be able to find the records and learn the full story. Until then, the Diocese treats this matter as though it were a state secret!

I also believe that more must be recorded about the Ramsay family and its time at Derbywood. Perhaps that will be the next project, but for now we have the history of the Old Glebe House from the time of first European settlement in the Grand Narrows district through to the present. And that is more than many people have.

Views of Pipers Cove in the early twentieth century, showing the community of Pipers Cove on the slopes of Briomachoal (UPPER PHOTO) and the former goverment wharf (LOWER PHOTO).
PUBLIC DOMAIN PHOTOGRAPHS

www.ingramcontent.com/pod-product-compliance
Lightning Source LLC
Chambersburg PA
CBHW030600080526
44585CB00012B/442